HOW TO ORGANIZE AND CLEAN YOUR HOME FOR ADULTS WITH ADHD

HOW TO ORGANIZE AND CLEAN YOUR HOME FOR ADULTS WITH ADHD

A COMPASSIONATE SYSTEM THAT HELPS ADULTS WITH ADHD TAME CLUTTER, BUILD HABITS, AND MAINTAIN A CALM HOME

ADHD LIFE SKILLS SERIES
BOOK 1

VERONICA HODGE

Copyright © 2025 by Veronica Hodge

All rights reserved.

No part of this publication may be reproduced, distributed, or transmitted in any form or by any means, including photocopying, recording, or other electronic or mechanical methods, without the prior written permission of the publisher, except in the case of brief quotations embodied in critical reviews and certain other noncommercial uses permitted by copyright law.

Disclaimer: The information provided in this book is for educational and entertainment purposes only. The author and publisher make no representation or warranties with respect to the accuracy, applicability, fitness, or completeness of the contents of this book. The information contained in this book is strictly for educational purposes. Therefore, if you wish to apply ideas contained in this book, you are taking full responsibility for your actions.

The author and publisher disclaim any warranties (express or implied), merchantability, or fitness for any particular purpose. The author and publisher shall in no event be held liable to any party for any direct, indirect, punitive, special, incidental, or other consequential damages arising directly or indirectly from any use of this material, which is provided "as is," and without warranties.

First Edition

To every reader who feels overwhelmed by clutter and the pull of perfection—this book is for you. May small, compassionate steps turn chaos into a home you can live in.

Not everything that is faced can be changed, but nothing can be changed until it is faced.

JAMES BALDWIN

CONTENTS

A Shame-Free Way to Get a Home That Works   xv

1. THE ADHD BRAIN AT HOME: MOTIVATION, FRICTION, AND DECISION FATIGUE   1
   Motivation Isn't Consistency   1
   Friction Mapping   5
   Decision Fatigue and Micro-Choices   8
   Time Blindness and Future You   11

2. START HERE: RESETTING THE PLAYING FIELD WITHOUT THE ALL-DAY CLEAN   15
   Quick Wins in Ten Minutes   15
   Clear Surfaces, Clear Minds   19
   Fast Triage: Trash, Dishes, Laundry   21
   Stop at the Good Enough Finish Line   24

3. BUILD YOUR ADHD-FRIENDLY CLEANING OPERATING SYSTEM   27
   Routines That Bend, Not Break   27
   Anchors That Trigger Action   31
   Rotations and Checklists to Lighten the Load   34
   The Two-Level Plan: Normal and Low-Energy Modes   38

4. BREAK TASKS DOWN WITHOUT MAKING A 47-STEP LIST   43
   The Smallest Possible Start   43
   Visual Chunking by Area   46
   Momentum Tools: Timers, Body Doubling, and Momentum   49
   End With a Setup Step   52

5. DECLUTTERING WITH ADHD: KEEP, TOSS, RELOCATE WITHOUT SPIRALING — 55
   Limits First, Less Clutter — 55
   Simple Rules, Clear Choices — 58
   Stop the Relocation Shuffle — 61
   Sentimental Clutter, Compassionate Care — 64

6. LAUNDRY THAT DOESN'T TAKE OVER YOUR LIFE — 69
   Simplify the Wardrobe and Supplies — 69
   Baskets, Zones, and Flow — 73
   Folding Alternatives — 77
   The Laundry Recovery Plan — 80

7. KITCHEN AND DISHES: FROM DOOM PILES TO DAILY USABILITY — 85
   Dish Minimums and Backup Plans — 85
   Countertop Rules That Stick — 89
   Fridge and Pantry Without Over-Organizing — 93
   Quick Clean Routines That Stick — 97

8. PAPERWORK, MAIL, AND DIGITAL CLUTTER: A SYSTEM YOU CAN TRUST — 103
   The Mail Triage Station — 103
   Simple Filing That Doesn't Require Perfection — 106
   Bills, Deadlines, and Automation — 109
   Digital Declutter Basics — 112

9. BEDROOMS, BATHROOMS, AND HIGH-FRICTION ZONES — 117
   Bedroom Launchpad: Start Here — 117
   Bathroom Reset Routines — 121
   Hot Spots and Drop Zones — 123
   Tools Where You Use Them — 126

10. LIVING WITH OTHERS: SHARED SPACES, BOUNDARIES, AND AGREEMENTS — 129
    Naming the Problem Without Blame — 129
    Clean Enough, Not Perfect: Shared Standards You Can Live With — 132

Play to Strengths: Task Division That Fits You	134
The Support Toolkit: Body Doubling, Check-ins, and Reminders	137
A Restartable Home and a Kinder Relationship With Cleaning	141

A SHAME-FREE WAY TO GET A HOME THAT WORKS

WHAT THIS BOOK IS (AND ISN'T)

From the moment you open this book, the goal is clear in a way that most organizing guides aren't: to reduce friction, reduce stress, and help you live with a home that works in real life, not a magazine spread. This book is for adults whose brains don't always play by the same rules the shelves of a home-improvement store assume. It's for the ADHD mind that often moves in bursts, loses time to distractions, and feels the pull of a thousand tiny decisions that never quite get resolved. If you've ever felt that organizing solutions come with a hidden demand you'll never meet, you're not alone. This book speaks to that exhaustion with a simple offer: start where you are, adjust as you go, and always be allowed to restart.

What this book is is a practical operating system you can customize. It is a toolkit of repeatable patterns rather than a rigid blueprint. It teaches you to design routines around your energy cycles, to create spaces that reduce friction, and to chunk tasks into steps that are small enough to begin even on the hardest days. The emphasis is on function, not perfection. We're aiming for a home that feels calmer and a life that feels sustainable, not a home that meets some external standard of "clean." The word clean here is a living concept—something that means calm, not flawless.

What this book isn't is a magic cure, a guilt trip, or a set of rules that assume you have unending time and pristine conditions. It isn't another checklist you can never complete. It isn't a personality-shaming pep talk that implies you should simply have more discipline if only you tried harder. Instead, it invites a different relationship with cleaning and organizing: one that recognizes the real constraints of attention, initiation, time perception, and fatigue, and responds with strategies that fit those realities.

You'll notice a through line across chapters: reduce friction. Every system, every habit, every space is designed to make the next action easier. You'll hear terms like *minimum viable actions, entry points,* and *the next right step* because those are the tools we use when motivation isn't reliable and planning feels paralyzing. There will be moments of deeper work and moments of tiny, achievable wins. Both are legitimate. The book is about building continuity rather than chasing heroic moments of productivity.

Who is this for? It's for adults with ADHD who want a home they don't dread every time they walk in the door. It's for partners, roommates, and families who share living spaces with someone who might experience tasks differently but still deserves a peaceful, usable home. It's for ADHD coaches and therapists who want a compassionate, practical resource to reference with clients who feel overwhelmed by traditional methods. It's for anyone tired of shame as a motivator and curious about an approach that respects energy, attention, and the unpredictable rhythms of real life.

How should you use it? Read in short bursts if you need to. Try a small change and live with it for a week before adding more. Notice what works, what doesn't, and why. Bring your own constraints into the design instead of pretending they don't exist. If a chapter speaks to you but you're in a different season of life than the example, adapt it gently. The aim isn't to complete every exercise perfectly but to cultivate a flexible, restartable way of living that makes home feel like support rather than stress.

This introduction holds a compact promise: you're not broken, you're human. Your brain handles priorities differently, and you deserve systems that respect that difference. The path you'll be invited to walk through this book is not a sprint. It's a practice—one that honors rest, momentum, and the messy, brilliant reality of living with ADHD.

WHY CLEANING FEELS HARD WITH ADHD

The challenges of cleaning and organizing don't spring from laziness or a lack of will. They're a direct reflection of how ADHD works inside the day-to-day reality of a home. Motivation, initiation, time perception, and decision fatigue interact in ways that turn small messes into overwhelming cliffs. When you understand the invisible forces at work, you gain a map for building systems that support you rather than fight you.

First, motivation in ADHD brains often follows momentum. The moment you begin a task, you may feel a spark that propels you forward. But that spark is fragile, easily snuffed by a single interruption, a sticky note of a new obligation, or the realization that the task will take longer than you want. The result is a cycle: start, stall, abandon, repeat. The cycle isn't evidence of character flaw; it's a mismatch between the way motivation often works and the way traditional cleaning plans demand consistency.

Initiation—the act of starting—is another tricky piece. Even simple chores can feel monumental if you're staring at a list of steps or a scene that feels unmanageable. When initiation is hard, procrastination isn't laziness as much as a system constraint. You need a doorway that's easy to step through, not a door that requires you to perform a full performance of perfection before you're allowed to begin.

Time perception, or time blindness, is another powerful force. The clock runs differently in ADHD brains. An hour can feel almost instantaneous, or it can stretch into forever if you're engaged by something else. This makes scheduling and estimating the duration of tasks unreliable. The result is a home that seems to drift away from you simply because the time you expected to invest never materializes.

Decision fatigue compounds everything. Each moment you decide what to do next—which item to keep, where to put it, which surface to tackle—you deplete cognitive energy. The more decisions you face, the harder the right decision becomes. For many people with ADHD, a single space can erupt into a decision avalanche that leaves them numb and still surrounded by clutter.

Sensory overwhelm also plays a role. Clutter isn't just visual; it's a cascade of sounds, textures, smells, and the mental noise of "what if." The mind can't filter it all effectively, and that overload makes even routine cleaning feel unsustainable. Space that's too busy or too loud can trigger shutdowns where nothing gets done, not because you don't want to, but because your nervous system needs a quieter, calmer invitation to engage.

Given these realities, what would help is a shift from fighting the ADHD brain to working with it. That means designing spaces and routines that require less energy to maintain, creating quick wins that build momentum, and letting go of standards that aren't practical for how your brain operates. It also means reframing what "clean" means in your home: clean can be the absence of daily chaos, the presence of a surface you can work on, the knowledge that you can find essential items without a scavenger hunt, and a sense that maintenance is a breathable practice rather than a heroic feat.

In this book, you'll see strategies that actively reduce friction: predictable cues, clearly defined next steps, and routines that align with your natural energy rhythms. You'll learn to trade perfection for reliability. You'll discover ways to lower the emotional cost of tidying and to reframe maintenance as a form of care—care for your space, your time, and your attention. The aim is not to erase all mess but to rewrite what it means for mess to matter: less chaos, more stability, and above all, options for choosing what you'll do next instead of what you feel forced to do.

HOW TO USE THIS BOOK WHEN YOU'RE ALREADY EXHAUSTED

Exhaustion changes the rules of every game, including the game of cleaning. When you're running on empty, the idea of a "deep tidy" can feel not only impossible but unnecessary. This section invites you to meet exhaustion where it lives—at the edge of the day, after a long meeting, during a hangover of fatigue, when your energy gauge shows red. The approach here is to provide entry points that are fast, visible, and repeatable. Think of them as gentle handholds you can grab without needing a sprint of motivation. The goal is to help you regain a sense of capability without pretending you can perform miracles on a bad day.

Start with small, visible wins. A single surface cleared, a trash emptied, a sink that looks a little brighter. These tiny results matter because they create momentum. When energy is low, the brain responds to tangible outcomes more readily than to grand plans. You don't have to complete a whole room to deserve a sense of progress. You just need to take the next right step that doesn't demand more energy than you have. A two-minute reset can be enough to re-establish a foothold. The next moment will come with its own possibilities, and sometimes that's enough to get you through another day.

On days when even the two-minute action feels out of reach, apply what I'll call the "recovery pause." Pause to name what you can do without turning the space upside down. There is enormous value in recognizing your limits and choosing the smallest action that still matters. Perhaps it's placing a single item back in its home, or wiping a single high-traffic surface with a damp cloth, or simply choosing to empty a trash can. The act of choosing, even for a moment, breaks the cycle of paralysis and resets the system for the next attempt.

To help make this workable, we'll rely on anchor habits that you can embed into your calendar and your routine. For instance, you might use a ritual of a five-minute reset at the end of the workday, when the house quiets down. The idea is not to cram in chores when you're exhausted but to offer a predictable, repeatable cue that you can follow without thinking too hard. You'll be taught to pair actions with cues you already have—when you brush your teeth, for example, you perform a quick wipe of the kitchen surface you use most often. Small pairs like this become micro-systems that accumulate over time.

Another essential idea is to build redundancy into your process. If one plan fails, you have a backup you can switch to without panic. On low-energy days, your backup might be a photographed checklist you can glance at instead of a mental list. It might be a small container where you drop tasks that you'll address later, so you know where to start when your energy returns. The point is not to push yourself into a state of constant "doing." It's to create a predictable, restartable pattern you can lean on when energy is scarce.

Finally, this book encourages you to treat your space as a living system that you're constantly tending, not a project with a fixed finish line. A living system adapts to the day's energy, to the season, and to your changing life. It's okay if what works this week won't work next month. The true measure of progress is not flawless performance but the ability to begin again with less shame and more clarity. When you're exhausted, your first job is to give yourself permission to rest, and your second job is to give yourself a tiny, doable doorway back into action.

SETTING YOUR PERSONAL DEFINITION OF "CLEAN ENOUGH"

A core claim of this book is that clean doesn't have to mean pristine. It means functional. It means a home that feels navigable, a space you can use without tripping over yourself, and a rhythm you can sustain without burning out. To find your own clean enough, you begin with a conversation with yourself about what you actually need to live well, given your energy, your body, and your household. This is not about lowering standards for ever; it is about recalibrating your standards so they match reality and thus become achievable.

Start by asking what really matters to you. Do you need counters clear enough to cook a meal without moving five items out of the way? Do you need a bed that is made once in a while, not every day? Do you need a calendar where you can find important papers in minutes rather than a scavenger hunt? These questions aren't about judgment; they are about clarity. When you know what matters, you can design habits around those anchors and let the rest drift with grace.

Next, translate values into concrete standards. Rather than a vague goal like "keep the kitchen clean," set a minimal standard that you can actually meet on a typical day. For example, "the sink is empty and wiped down at the end of the day," or "the laundry room is tidy enough that I can start a load without shuffling through a pile." These statements become the yardsticks you measure yourself against. They are intentionally narrow so they don't demand heroic discipline, yet they are specific enough to be meaningful.

As you define clean enough, consider the realities of your living situation. If you share space with someone else, factor in their needs and rhythms as part of the standard rather than as a constraint you must overcome alone. The goal is shared clarity, not silent resentment. You can build agreements that honor both your needs and theirs. You may decide that a shared surface should be free of clutter by a certain time each day, or that a weekly reset will occur at a predictable moment when everyone's routines align. The boundaries you set should feel fair, practical, and sustainable.

Part of setting your personal standard is building a plan for the inevitable days when you fall short. Instead of spiraling, you give yourself permission to restart. The question to carry forward is not "Did I achieve perfection?" but "What's the smallest next action that can restore order in this space?" Your answer becomes a daily compass, not a verdict.

To make this concrete in your life, take a moment to write a short personal definition of clean enough for one space you care about—the kitchen, your desk, your bedroom, or a shared area. Include a few sentences about what a functioning version of that space looks like, how long you're willing to invest on a given day, and what you'll do when you're running on empty. Then imagine the space as a living system that can be tuned over time. Your definition may shift with the seasons, with a change in living arrangements, or with new energy patterns. That flexibility is not a weakness; it's a practical adaptation to a real life.

As you settle on your own standard, you'll begin to see cleaning not as a moral test but as a practice of care for your environment and your attention. You'll learn to value progress over perfection and to design your routines around the person you are today, not the person you wish to be tomorrow. This book will help you carry that definition forward as a living guide—one that you can restart, adjust, and rely on again and again.

ONE
THE ADHD BRAIN AT HOME: MOTIVATION, FRICTION, AND DECISION FATIGUE

MOTIVATION ISN'T CONSISTENCY

Motivation in an ADHD brain isn't a steady drumbeat you must march to every day. It's a pulse that speeds up and slows down, sometimes with the suddenness of a horn blast, sometimes with the gentle fading of a sunset. The old idea that motivation equals consistency is a myth that leaves a lot of people feeling disappointed, then ashamed, then defeated. When you're navigating clutter and chores, you're not failing to be consistent; you're riding the natural rhythms of interest, novelty, urgency, and reward. And once you understand that, you can design systems that ride those rhythms instead of fighting them.

Think of motivation as a signal rather than a command. Your attention is drawn to things that feel new, useful, or urgent. You might find yourself eagerly folding a favorite shirt when you're in the mood for a quick win, or you might sprint through a pile of mail the moment a timer starts because the moment feels charged with the urgency of a deadline you didn't know you had. The trick is to map those signals and shape your tasks to align with them, rather than waiting for a top-down drive that may never arrive on a given day.

In practice this means reframing how you choose what to do. A task that feels dull can still become doable if you attach it to something that sparks interest, or if the end of the task promises a crisp, tangible result. A tiny, almost laughably small win—like setting a jar for sorted receipts and discovering that you can see the bottom of the jar within minutes—can trigger enough momentum to carry you a little farther. Your brain does not require heroic acts; it needs clear, meaningful steps that end with a visible payoff.

This approach also invites a gentler relationship with failure. If a day passes with little progress, that is information, not verdict. You can use that information to design for tomorrow rather than berating yourself about today. The energy and attention you bring to a space is a moving target, and that means your systems must be adaptable, forgiving, and specific enough to actually work when your focus flickers.

A practical way to implement this is to structure tasks around micro-wins that feel rewarding immediately.

When you wake up and survey the kitchen, you can choose a start that is inherently attractive. Maybe it's the chance to reclaim your surface from the menace of paper: you set a tiny boundary, like clearing one small counter tile and smoothing a few stacks into a neat pile. The moment you see that tidy line, your brain registers a reward—proof that your efforts have a real, visible effect. You don't need a grand transformation to begin; you need a moment of clarity and a next right step that you can begin without a long prelude.

Another lever is novelty. Even though you won't reinvent your whole home each day, you can refresh the frame around a familiar task. Rename routines to give them a narrative. Instead of "clean the kitchen," you might think of it as "mission: clear the counter" or "speed round: dishes before a show." The new frame creates a sense of play that your ADHD brain often craves. You can also pair tasks with short, upcoming moments you look forward to —like a favorite podcast, a moment of quiet with tea after you finish, or a quick chat with a friend when you've hit a small milestone.

Urgency, properly harnessed, can be a friend rather than a tyrant. Set a timer for a small, bounded window and declare a defined end point. The alarm becomes both a cue and a boundary. You're not racing against time so much as inviting time to cooperate with you. The sense of urgency is built into the environment, not demanded of your willpower alone. You'll notice that on days when you're already energized, you can lean into a slightly bigger task with confidence, and on days when energy is scarce, you'll still find a meaningful, limited objective that won't collapse under its own weight.

Rewards deserve careful attention. They aren't bribes that undermine your integrity; they're cognitive anchors that reinforce a pattern you want to repeat. A small reward after a micro-win can be as simple as pausing to stretch, stepping outside for a breath of air, or giving yourself a moment to check a message that matters to you. The key is to keep rewards proportional to the effort and to avoid letting the reward become the sole reason for doing the task. The best rewards leave you with a sense of closure, not a temporary distraction that sends you spinning into a new mess.

In the end, motivation, for the ADHD brain, is about creating a cascade of tiny successes that accumulate over time. It's not a sign of weakness when you struggle with consistency; it's a signal that your environment and your choices aren't designed to support your unique tempo. The work you do—whether it's folding a load of laundry, sorting mail, or starting a new cleaning station—becomes sustainable when you attach it to things you already care about, or can care about almost immediately. The long view still matters, but the way you move through it is built from opt-in moments, quick wins, and a few well-timed surprises that remind you that progress is possible today, not someday, and that someday can start now.

FRICTION MAPPING

Friction is the word we use for every little obstacle that makes a task feel heavier than it is. It's the distance between intention and action, the moment your brain starts weighing the costs of starting rather than enjoying the benefit of completing. In homes with ADHD, friction isn't a moral failing; it's the real physics of attention, memory, and motion colliding with imperfect systems. The first step toward change is to name friction honestly, then to redesign the space and routines so that starting feels almost too easy to resist.

To map friction, begin by choosing a zone where you want to see improvement. It could be the entryway that explodes with clutter after a workday, the kitchen counters that accumulate a sort of ecological drift, or the laundry area where clothes seem to multiply when you're not looking. Observe as if you're a scientist in your own home. Watch what you reach for first when you decide to tidy. Notice how many times you must decide what to do next, and how often you have to fetch something you forgot you needed. Listen for the mental refrains that pop up—oh, I'll do it later, I'll do it when I have time, I need the right container, I'll start after this episode ends. Each refrain is a friction point that your future self would like you to remove.

Friction shows up in patterns. Distance matters. If the bin you need is across the room, you'll do a mental calculation that ends in inaction. If the detergent is tucked away behind a cabinet you don't open often, you'll avoid starting because you don't want to dig for it. The number of steps to complete a task matters as much as the lot of decisions you must make along the way. A pile of clothes isn't just a pile; it's a decision-maker that whispers that this space requires a big, heroic effort. Tools matter too. If your basic cleaning supplies live in a single, portable caddy by the door, you're far more likely to sweep through a space before you've overthought your approach.

Once you start mapping, you begin to see a web of small adjustments that add up. A landing zone near the door where you drop mail and keys prevents the swirl of clutter from migrating into the living spaces. A simple caddy with all the "everyday" laundry tools—detergent, dryer sheet, a pair of scissors, a small brush for lint—turns a nightly task into a quick, nearly effortless routine. A dedicated trash bag in the laundry room, an empty hamper on the bedroom floor, a folded towel at the sink—these tiny fixtures become invisible rails that guide you toward action instead of resistance.

The clever part of friction mapping is that it rewards modest changes. You don't have to overhaul your entire house to gain traction. You only need to remove enough friction so that starting is the moment of decision rather than a struggle that drags on. When you map friction honestly, you discover the friction you never noticed before: the moment you realize you don't actually need that tool today, or the surprise that a single magnetic hook in a new place makes a distant task suddenly possible. You begin to see that your space is not a battlefield but a set of sympathetic design choices that can support you when your energy and attention are fluctuating.

As you map, you'll also learn to anticipate recurring friction. You may find that laundry always feels like a sprint after work; therefore a small, consistent routine in that zone can prevent the disarray from piling up. Or you might realize that paperwork tends to explode when you're tired, so you design a tiny, ritualistic processing sequence that you can perform with minimal cognitive load. The point isn't to eliminate all friction but to engineer friction in a way that invites action rather than paralyzes it.

Friction mapping is best done with a gentle posture. Be curious about what slows you down rather than punitive about what you fail to move today. The aim is to reduce the number of small decisions you must make in a single moment, so your brain can use its energy for actual problem-solving rather than for mental gatekeeping. The reward for this patient work is a home that feels navigable again, a space where you see an option and you can take it without negotiating with every competing impulse inside your head.

DECISION FATIGUE AND MICRO-CHOICES

Decision fatigue is the quiet thief at the edge of a tidy morning. It chips away at the energy you have left after a day of making choices, and for many adults with ADHD, the daily stream of small selections becomes a canyon. The brain loves defaults, but ADHD minds often drift toward options that feel more stimulating or urgent. When too many micro-choices accumulate, tidying stalls out, and the mess quietly resumes control. The intervention is not to somehow summon heroic willpower but to redesign the day so that the right decision is the easy one.

A core principle is to reduce the number of choices you must actively make. You can do this by building routines that are predictable and flexible at the same time. Predictability gives your brain a map to follow; flexibility ensures you don't feel trapped when energy shifts. The moment you have a reliable sequence, you can move through it with less cognitive load, leaving energy for the moments that truly matter.

Consider the rhythm of a space you want to tame, such as a kitchen that slips into a doom pile after every meal. Instead of a grand plan that depends on a perfect mood, you can establish a simple, repeatable pattern: wipe a surface and sweep one small corner after you finish cooking, then rinse and load the dishwasher before you sit down. The routine is not a punishment; it's a dance with your energy, designed so that you can glide through it even when your attention is flitting around. The key is to anchor the routine to existing habits—the moment you finish a coffee, the moment a show ends, the moment you step back from a screen. The routine becomes almost automatic because it's tethered to something you already do.

Another facet of micro-choices is to create a curated set of options you can rely on without rereading the menu. If you always start with a particular action, such as clearing the coffee table, you'll train your brain to default to a clean baseline. The next right step is then waiting for you, not waiting for you to wrestle with it. The power of a micro-choice lies in its intensity: something small enough to begin immediately yet meaningful enough to move you toward a calmer space. This is where the idea of a restart-friendly system shines. It's okay to stop after a tiny win and pick up again later; the system doesn't punish you for restarts. It adapts to your pace, and you adapt with it.

Decision fatigue also factors in the presence of options you didn't anticipate. A messy closet offers dozens of possible actions, some of them contradictory. Your task is to reduce the field of play. Keep a single, obvious path forward in a zone. In laundry, that might mean a dedicated hamper system with one color-coded load for one cycle, nothing more. In paperwork, a single inbox for new items and a separate processing area for existing piles minimizes the dance of decisions. When there are fewer routes to consider, you can choose quickly and move on, and the brain can allocate its remaining bandwidth to more complex problems that actually demand attention.

A useful cognitive move is to create a ceiling for decision-making within a given period. For example, you set a limit on how long you will deliberate before starting a task. You decide that when you sit down with a goal, you won't permit yourself to ruminate for more than a minute; after that, you pick the next right step you can start within the next minute. The point isn't to suppress thought but to prevent paralysis by analysis. If you need to adjust the zone, you adjust. If you need a different default, you set a new one. Your system should be as restart-friendly as it is durable, able to bend without breaking when life throws a curveball.

The social layer matters, too. You can enlist others as accountability allies, not as judges. A partner or housemate can become a gentle co-pilot of your micro-choices by offering a quick check-in or by providing a shared cue that you've agreed upon. The goal is not to police yourself into perfection but to design a shared rhythm that reduces friction in everyday life. When the space you share reinforces your defaults rather than constantly challenging them, you experience less cognitive drag and more steady momentum.

What you'll discover as you practice is that decision fatigue isn't something to fear. It's a signpost that tells you where to simplify. Your job is to design a landscape in which your decisions are small, fast, and aligned with your energy. You're not trying to eliminate all friction or remove all uncertainty. You're trying to create predictable, forgiving channels through which your focus can travel and complete a task with dignity and ease.

TIME BLINDNESS AND FUTURE YOU

Time is a slippery thing for many adults with ADHD. The clock seems to run at its own pace, and the future you who will benefit from an organized space often lives in a different dimension of time altogether. Time blindness makes it hard to estimate how long tasks will take, to remember to start, and to imagine how a current mess will feel once someone interrupts you with a new distraction. The result is a cycle of underestimation, overestimation, postponement, and reactive work that leaves you exhausted, even if you've spent hours "doing something." The antidote is not more discipline but clearer time cues, anchored routines, and a compassionate approach to your future self.

One foundational idea is to replace vague estimates with concrete landmarks. Instead of promising to tidy the kitchen for an hour, you can anchor the plan to a duration that matches your energy level and your environment: a 15-minute sprint after you finish a meal, or a 20-minute window just before your favorite show. The goal is to give your brain something finite to negotiate with, something that feels doable and real, not theoretical. You can pair that time frame with a visible cue in the room—an hourglass on the counter, a digital timer that ticks in the corner of your vision, or a lamp that shifts color when the window opens. The cue becomes the organizer, pulling your attention back to the current moment rather than letting it drift toward endless possibilities of tomorrow.

A related tactic is to embed time-bound rituals into the day. A ritual is not a rigid schedule; it is a gentle, reliable habit that marks transition from one activity to another. For example, you can designate a "transition minute" after work: you step into the kitchen, set a timer, and choose one small task you know you'll complete within that minute. If you've had a brutally long day, you still finish that minute with something tangible—a folded towel, a cleared counter, a mail stack reduced by a single pass. The ritual is the heartbeat of your time management, a signal to your brain that the moment is ripe for action.

Time blindness also benefits from secondary cues that help your future self understand the consequences of present actions. A simple strategy is to place a small, visible reminder on the spot where the task happens. A clipboard with a single line of decision rules resting on the kitchen counter becomes the decision guide for the day. A sticky note on the entry table that says "Did you start the load?" acts as a micro-prompt that nudges you toward action at the right moment. These cues do not nag; they align with your cognitive pattern, offering a gentle reminder at the moment you typically drift.

There is power in creating visible progress. A wall-mounted chart with little progress tokens can give you a sense of movement at the speed your brain can handle. Each token represents a completed micro-task rather than a grand, all-encompassing victory. The satisfaction of moving a token can be enough to propel you forward into the next small action, and the moment you realize you're not merely keeping up but building forward momentum becomes a turning point in your relationship with time.

Another crucial piece is designing for "Future You." The person who will exist after you finish the task is a real, anticipatory agent in your planning. You can ask Future You what would help them breathe more easily: a clean kitchen after dinner, a bed that is made every morning, a desk with a single, clear surface. When you design with Future You in mind, you create rules that your future self can and will enforce. You set up the environment to reduce the chances of forgetting or backsliding. That might mean laying out the exact tools you will need for a given task the night before or prebooking a small block of time in your calendar for a weekly reset—a sustainable, low-friction anchor rather than a heroic, one-off sprint.

If you get nothing else from this chapter, take with you the idea that time management is not about forcing a perfect schedule but about aligning your spaces, choices, and cues with how your brain processes time. Your steps don't have to be large to be meaningful. Small, repeatable actions anchored in clear cues create a rhythm your future self can trust. When you treat Future You as a legitimate partner in your cleaning journey, you release much of the frustration that comes from trying to manage time with only present-moment attention. You build a home that adjusts to your tempo rather than requiring you to adjust to an abstract ideal of what a tidy space should look like.

TWO
START HERE: RESETTING THE PLAYING FIELD WITHOUT THE ALL-DAY CLEAN

QUICK WINS IN TEN MINUTES

If your space feels like a traffic jam of consequences, a ten-minute reset can be a lifeline. You don't need momentum to start; you only need a moment where you decide that the space will be usable again, even if only for a little while. For many people with ADHD, the roadblock isn't a lack of desire but the enormity of the next thing to do. The idea of an all-day deep clean can feel distant, intimidating, or even impossible. A ten-minute reset meets that moment where it hurts, then gives you something you can actually accomplish within your current energy and attention window. The goal isn't to solve everything at once. It's to restore enough order to reduce cognitive load, to create a visible win, and to show your brain that starting is possible again tomorrow. This is about momentum, not perfection.

Choose a single area that tugged at you most this morning, last night, or the moment you opened the door. A coffee table cluttered with magazines, a kitchen counter you pass every day, or the floor near the entry where shoes vanish into a pile every time you walk in. The act is simple: set a timer for ten minutes, and give yourself permission to stop when the bell rings. In those ten minutes you're aiming for a coherent, usable state, not a pristine one. Remove obvious trash and put it in a bin you keep near the area. Gather items that belong elsewhere and relocate them in a single pass rather than chasing every stray item around the house. Put things back in their homes as long as the home is readily reachable, and then let the rest rest for the moment. If something is beyond quick repair—stains that require soaking, cords tangled into a knot, files that need sorting—you acknowledge them, but you don't solve them in this burst. You tag them as a future task and return to the present task at hand.

As you begin, listen for cues from your body and your environment. If your breathing is shallow and your heart feels loud, you're probably looking at more friction than you can absorb with ten minutes. In that case, scale down to eight minutes or switch to a different area that feels lighter. The point is to build a habit of small, repeatable wins. If your space has a lot of visible clutter, a quick triage mindset helps you pick the right target: start with anything that blocks the space from being used. A starlight moment can happen when you clear the coffee table and see the surface you can work with again, which in turn makes it easier to imagine cooking a simple meal or sitting down with a book without a mental avalanche following you.

In practice, the ten-minute reset can look like this: you scan the area, notice trash that needs disposal, and act quickly to bag it. Then you identify items that don't belong on the surface and either relocate them to a proper home or place them in a temporary resting place for sorting later. A shallow wipe of the surface can be enough to reclaim its usability; you don't have to polish a table, you just clear it. If you have a sink nearby, you might load a few dishes into it, rinse and stack them in a way that makes the sink usable again, and set a small intention for tomorrow—perhaps to run the dishwasher first thing in the morning or to unload the sink before you start your day. If there's a light floor you can vacuum or sweep in ten minutes, do a quick sweep instead of dragging out a heavy cleaning session. The point is to end with a space that physically feels lighter and more navigable, a space that your brain can register as a habitat rather than a hazard.

Sometimes your ten-minute window will feel too short, and that's okay. The strategy is to begin with a tiny commitment you can honor. If you finish early, you earned a second win—an extra burst of momentum that you can bank for tomorrow. If you don't finish, you still gained something tangible: you've interrupted the downward spiral of piling and you've created a container in which it feels possible to start again. The trick is to treat the ten-minute reset as a regular, repeatable ritual rather than a one-off event. Mark the space as "in progress" with a simple sign or a designated tray so you can resume without ruminating for hours about what's left. As you practice, you'll learn which areas are most forgiving in ten minutes and which require smaller, more frequent resets. Either way, you'll collect a sequence of quick wins that accumulate into a noticeably calmer home and a more hopeful relationship with chores.

Finally, consider pairing the ten-minute reset with a tiny accountability ritual. Tell a friend, partner, or roommate that you'll send a quick check-in after you finish, or leave a simple note on the space—something like: "Surface cleared, next steps tomorrow." The external nudge can be surprisingly powerful in breaking the inertia that ADHD brains often carry. The ten-minute reset isn't about doing less; it's about doing something sustainable with the energy you have. When you finish, pause, breathe, acknowledge the win, and tell yourself that this becomes your new baseline. The next reset will be easier because you've already proven to yourself that a small commitment can yield a visible, meaningful change.

CLEAR SURFACES, CLEAR MINDS

When a room feels usable, your brain feels invited to move, to think, to plan. The rule is simple in its instinct: clear the surfaces first, because a clean countertop or a bare coffee table acts like a pause button for your stress. Surfaces are like the dashboards of our living spaces. They collect light, color, and motion, or they absorb it in a way that makes the room feel heavier. On ADHD days—days of racing thoughts, wavering motivation, and decision fatigue—surface clutter can act like a low-grade alarm, reminding you of all the things you haven't yet decided about yourself and your space. Losing the mental energy to decide what to do next often starts with what you see right now. Clear surfaces first, and you buy yourself the cognitive bandwidth to decide later with less resistance.

This approach isn't about perfection or about having the cleanest house on the block. It's about creating a stable, functional backdrop for your life. Start by identifying the surfaces that repeatedly trap items: the kitchen counters where mail, groceries, and takeout land; the coffee table in the living room that gathers remotes, cups, and magazines; the entryway shelf where keys, mail, and bags linger. These aren't moral tests; they are friction points—the places that announce, through clutter, that you haven't finished your last decision. The goal is to reduce that friction enough to calm the brain's signal that says: there's more to do than I can handle right now.

Once you've chosen a surface, practice a simple ritual to reclaim it. Look at what is there, then decide: will this stay, go somewhere else, or get a temporary home for now? If something belongs somewhere else but you're not ready to put it there, place it in a clearly labeled temporary spot you can return to in the same day. If something is trash or a recyclables item, move it immediately to the correct bin, then wipe the surface clean with a quick pass of a cloth or wipe. The wipe doesn't have to be perfect; it just needs to remove the visible residue that makes the space feel chaotic. The sense of closure comes from completing one pass and standing back to observe the difference. The surface is no longer a visual drumbeat of unfinished business; it's a line drawn in the sand that says, for now, this space is usable.

In practice, the clear surfaces approach often shifts your room's energy in unexpected ways. A kitchen counter that was once a catch-all becomes a place where you can lay out ingredients and prepare a simple meal. A coffee table that always looks crowded now hosts a single bowl of remotes and a plant, which immediately reduces the psychic noise in the room. An entryway that used to trip you up with a floating bag is now predictable: you drop keys in a bowl, set a mail tray on a mat, and know that you can walk through the door without the mental tax of deciding where to put things each time you come home. The change is subtle, but the effect is cumulative. With fewer items on the surface, you can see the room's furniture, texture, and lighting more clearly, and that altered perception often triggers calmer, more intentional behavior.

To keep this momentum, designate one surface in each room as the "surface-keeping zone." This is where you resist the impulse to heap, stack, or stash. Everything you place there must be essential to the space's use or must have a clear home. If you're unsure whether something belongs, it probably doesn't. When you walk into a room and notice that the surface remains clear, your brain registers a win before you've even started moving. The first impression you make on yourself each day carries disproportionate weight; clear surfaces improve that first impression and invite you to continue with gentler, more doable tasks. In this way, the rule becomes a habit: you don't waste energy arguing with clutter that's already out of sight; you avoid creating new friction by keeping key surfaces available for the everyday actions of living. The result is not a perfectly ordered home but a home that respects your ADHD brain's need for clarity, rhythm, and a sense of control over your environment.

FAST TRIAGE: TRASH, DISHES, LAUNDRY

The fast triage approach treats space like a river that can overflow if you don't intervene quickly enough. In ADHD thinking, tasks tend to multiply. A trash can becomes a trash avalanche; dishes left in the sink invite more dishes to pile up; laundry left in a basket can become a tower that feels insurmountable. The fast triage is a way to interrupt that multiplication by hitting the three biggest accelerants of mess—trash, dishes, and laundry—before they gain momentum. The aim is not to complete a perfect round of cleaning but to create a new order that is easy to maintain and hard to undo in a single afternoon. This is where decisiveness meets practicality. You're choosing quick, high-impact actions that reduce both physical clutter and decision fatigue. You're not chasing a spotless home; you're creating a dependable rhythm that feels manageable regardless of how you're feeling that day.

Begin with trash. A bag or bin stands as the first line of defense. It's the quickest way to reclaim a space because trash is the most destructive amplifier of disorganization: it makes surfaces slippery with disappointment and fills air with lingering smells that slow you down. If you can locate a bag or bin near the area, you can seal the disturbance in seconds, and the space immediately looks lighter. Dishes come next. The sink, the drainboard, or the dish rack becomes your central command for returning foodware to order. You shift from chaos to function by rinsing, stacking, and placing items in the dishwasher or on their way to the office or pantry if they need relocation. A single pass through the dishes can free up counter space, reduce the cognitive load of visual clutter, and give you a mental checkpoint that you can carry into a future session. Finally, laundry asserts its own gravity. Even a small load, begun and placed into a washer or dryer, offers a concrete completion signal: progress is happening, day after day, even when motivation is uneven. If you're tired of folding, consider a lightweight compromise: pull clothes from the dryer when they're still a bit warm, shake out wrinkles, and put them into a hamper or a basket for a future folding session. The key is to start a cycle, not to finish every garment perfectly. The act of starting creates a feedback loop: you'll see the results the next time you walk by, and you'll be more likely to continue.

In practice, you might find yourself in the kitchen with a sink full of dishes and a counter that doubles as a landing zone for mail and grocery bags. You begin by picking up every piece of trash you can reach, letting nothing rest in a landfill of neglect. Then you move to the dishes, clearing space in the sink and restoring a functional rhythm to meal preparation. Finally you address laundry, starting a load and getting it spinning while you tackle something else, so you feel the momentum without having to devote the day to one cycle. It's a triage that respects ADHD realities: quick, visible wins that prevent the mess from compounding and that leave you with a clear, clean baseline to build on tomorrow.

This approach also acknowledges that some days you won't complete all three categories in a single burst. That's acceptable. The crucial part is to have an established routine that you can repeat and tweak. The simple truth is that trash removal, dish management, and a small laundry cycle can reduce the cognitive drag enough to let you think more clearly about the next right action. By handling the three pressure points in a single pass, you change the layout of your day in ways you can recognize and sustain. You'll notice that the room feels lighter, your breathing becomes easier, and you're more willing to engage with other tasks that you've been putting off. The fast triage is not a one-off trick; it's a foundational habit you can rely on even when your energy dips, your schedule shifts, or your mood fluctuates. It's about building a space that can support you instead of defeating you.

STOP AT THE GOOD ENOUGH FINISH LINE

A common trap for people with ADHD is that finishing never feels finished. The look of the space can scream "not done," and the mental pressure to push through can produce a shutdown rather than sustainable progress. The idea of stopping at a good enough finish line flips the script. It's not about settling for a messy outcome; it's about choosing a boundary that honors your energy and your brain's current state while still making the space usable enough to live in and return to later. A good enough finish line gives you permission to pause with intention, to close a session with a clear, repeatable signal, and to carry momentum into the next moment rather than saturating your day with guilt and perfectionism.

The finish line is a boundary you set ahead of time, a moment when you can honestly say, I have done enough for now. It could be a visible completion—surface cleared, a practical category put away, a space that feels navigable again. It could be a time-based limit—ten minutes, thirty minutes, an agreed window with your household—whatever makes sense for your energy pattern and your responsibilities. The key is that the finish line signals a transfer of focus from the space to the plan for tomorrow. You leave the room with a clear sense of what you've accomplished and a concrete next step to begin the next time you enter. This is where the magic of restartability lives. If you walk away with a plan for the next step and a sense that the space is safe to re-enter, you've won.

To make this work, create a closing ritual that is easy to repeat. It might be a ritual of ritual: a quick wipe of the surfaces you touched, a brief check that every item has a home (or a designated temporary home with a note to relocate later), and a small log of what you accomplished that day. For many people with ADHD, a simple note or a photo can become a tactile reminder of progress, a reference point for the next reset. The emotional weight of cleaning shifts when you can look back on what you did, rather than fixating on what remains. The good enough finish line also invites you to plan your next step with a critical but compassionate lens. What is the smallest additional action that would push you forward the moment you wake up tomorrow? Perhaps it's taking the empty dish tub to the sink first, or placing a mail tray by the door so you can sort mail on your way out. The idea is to anchor your future action with a clearly defined next right step that doesn't demand a perfect script or a flawless routine.

Throughout this chapter, the goal has been to replace the binary of "clean or dirty" with a practical scale of usability. Good enough is not a surrender; it's a strategic stance that preserves energy for the next decision while preserving dignity and reduce friction. In the long run, this stance helps you build a living system that adapts to changing energy levels, shifting schedules, and the inevitable ups and downs of life with ADHD. When you end a session with a clear finish line, you leave with a sense of closure and readability that you can translate into tomorrow's practice. The space becomes a partner in your day rather than a source of anxiety. And that is the heart of an ADHD-friendly cleaning plan: a steady, restartable rhythm that fits you, not a perfect, one-time transformation that demands everything all at once.

THREE
BUILD YOUR ADHD-FRIENDLY CLEANING OPERATING SYSTEM

ROUTINES THAT BEND, NOT BREAK

Routines are not rigid chains. They are flexible scaffolds you can lean on when energy falters. For ADHD brains, routines work best when they are small, concrete, and repeatable. You don't aim for perfection across the whole house; you design a few essential rhythms that create visible relief and then let them flex with your week. A good routine honors the reality that motivation ebbs and attention wanders. The goal is to reduce decision fatigue by turning a handful of actions into a familiar pipeline you can step into without debating every move. Start by naming the outcomes that would most reduce stress if they happened every day. For many people, those outcomes are simple: a kitchen counter you can actually use, laundry that doesn't sit in a basket for days, mail that doesn't multiply into a small mountain, and a bathroom that feels clean enough to start the day. Once you know the outcomes, you design routines around the cues that naturally occur in your life. The cue could be something as ordinary as finishing your morning coffee, stepping out of the shower, or returning home after work. The cue doesn't have to be dramatic; it just needs to be consistent enough that you can expect it every day. Then you decide the smallest action you can take that will move you toward the outcome and make that action easy to do in the moment. A routine is not a long checklist; it is a single, reliable push in the right direction, just enough to create momentum. The smallest action matters because it lowers the barrier to starting, and starting is the hardest part for many ADHD brains. Once the first action is done, the rest tends to unfold with more ease than you expect. A practical rule of thumb is to pick routines that can be completed in five minutes or less on a typical day. If you discover you can't keep within five minutes, you're likely choosing too many steps or too much friction. The aim is momentum, not punishment. When you keep the steps tiny, you can do them on the days when energy feels like a slow drip, and you can still finish with a sense of progress. This is how you build a system that survives bad weeks. Routines that bend instead of break stay intact through memory gaps, fatigue, and the occasional meltdown of motivation. They're not perfect; they're repeatable. They're designed so that if you miss a day, you don't have to restart from scratch. You simply pick up where you left off, or you scale back to a version that fits today's energy.

The most successful routines are anchored in what you already do, not in what you wish you did. They piggyback on existing patterns and turn them into a reliable current rather than a creaky ladder you slip from whenever the winds change. Begin by selecting two or three core routines that cover the most frequent friction points in your home. Perhaps one routine seals the kitchen's daily work—clearing the counter, rinsing a few dishes, and starting a load in the dishwasher. Another routine might be a quick evening reset that clears the clutter from the living room floor, sets a timer for five minutes, and places a few essential items back in their homes. The third routine could be a daily quick-purge of paper or mail clutter at a consistent time, so piles don't gather into a storm. With each routine, articulate the smallest possible action you can take to move toward the outcome, and write down the cue that will prompt you to start. The best routines are simply the next right small thing, not a grand, perfect plan. Try a habit-stacking approach where you couple a routine with an existing habit. If you brush your teeth after waking up, could you also start a load of laundry or wipe down the kitchen counter at that moment? If you come home and put down your keys, could you spend the next two minutes putting things away and turning on the living room light? Habit stacking helps your brain see a connection between two familiar actions, making the second action feel almost automatic. It is crucial to allow for variability. Bad weeks will happen, and that is precisely why your routines must be resilient. If you miss your morning routine because you slept late, you still have a second routine you can perform in the afternoon or evening that yields similar relief. The aim is not a flawless cadence but a dependable rhythm that your life can accommodate. To keep momentum, set up gentle, non-punishing resets that help you restart without shame. For instance, if you wake up and realize you slept through your normal routine, you can trigger a "two-step reset" later in the day: first, wash your face and drink water; second, choose the simplest action that touches your most urgent friction point, like starting a load of laundry or sorting a single pile of mail. This approach preserves your dignity and your energy, turning the day's effort into a series of small, doable wins. A misstep should not derail the entire day. It should prompt a quick reevaluation and a fresh start, with clear, low-cost steps forward. Think of your routines as elastic: they stretch to accommodate your choices, but they don't snap when pressure increases. In practice, this means naming your non-negotiables and then designing adaptable routes to meet them. Your non-negotiables might be that the kitchen is usable by the end of the day, that laundry finds a rhythm rather than turning into a crisis, and that mail clutter does not pile up beyond recognition. The way you reach those goals is by keeping the plan human: you choose actions that are realistically integrable into your energy, your schedule, and your tolerance for structure. As you experiment, you'll start to notice what helps most: routines you can plug into days with brisk energy, and alternate versions you can lean on when energy drops. The point is not to chase perfect performance but to build a simple, repeatable framework that steadily reduces friction and builds trust in your own system. Remember that the objective is a calmer home life, not a flawless one. If you can create a predictable rhythm around a handful of essential tasks, you will experience fewer moments of panic or shame, and you will find yourself restarting with less resistance after setbacks. The framework you're building is not a prison; it is a portable toolkit you carry into every room and every season of life. It should feel doable, even when you're tired, overwhelmed, or dealing with the unpredictable edges of ADHD. The more you practice, the more the routine becomes automatic, and the more you begin to notice the unexpected benefits—a lighter mental load, better sleep, clearer mornings, and a home that reflects your life rather than your lapses.

ANCHORS THAT TRIGGER ACTION

Anchors work because they connect a useful task to a moment that already exists in your day. They reduce decision fatigue by turning choices into reactions. For many people with ADHD, a large portion of the struggle around cleaning is not trouble with the task itself but trouble with starting. An anchor is a friendly prompt that says, in effect, It's time to do this now, because you're already in a place where you can act. The beauty of anchors is that they don't require extra planning on days when energy is scarce. They ride along with routines that you already perform, and they multiply the chances that you will begin the next right action. Start by mapping a few reliable moments in your day that feel non-negotiable or nearly universal. The moment you finish your coffee, the moment you step out of the shower, the moment you return from work, or the moment you sit down to answer mail are all opportunities to pair a task with a cue. The cue itself is not a demand; it's a signal that a small, specific step is waiting for you. When you choose your anchors, prioritize cues that you encounter consistently and that require minimal friction to act on. The linked task should be small yet meaningful enough that completing it creates a noticeable improvement in your space. For example, the anchor after a shower could be to wipe down the bathroom counter and put away towels. The anchor after returning home could be a two-minute reset: remove shoes, hang a coat, and start a load of laundry or sort mail. The anchor after you brew coffee could be to place dirty dishes in the sink or rinse a weekend coffee mug and wipe the countertop. The key is to keep the action tiny and specific. It should be something you can do without gathering a lot of supplies or making a complicated plan. The more you see the immediate payoff, the more likely you are to repeat it. Another crucial element of anchors is visibility. Put the cue and the next action where you will see it. A sticky note on the bathroom mirror or a gentle reminder on your phone can serve as a cue itself, reinforcing the habit. Visual prompts do two jobs at once:

they remind you what to do and remind you of why this matters. If your space becomes a place where you feel pressure instead of relief, reframe the anchor. It should invite you to act, not punish you for not acting sooner. For example, if a particular shelf always becomes a dumping ground, place a single bin on the floor nearby and create a zero-silence rule: every item returned to the room must be placed inside that bin for sorting later. This makes the process less about policing yourself and more about creating an orderly path of least resistance. Anchors also benefit from being paired with simple rewards, especially at the start. The reward doesn't have to be grand; it can be a brief moment of appreciation, a stretch break, or a few minutes of listening to a favorite song while you work. The idea is to train your brain to associate the action with a positive mood or a small interruption that you enjoyed. The reward should be modest and immediate, so it reinforces the behavior in the moment rather than in the long run. The truth about anchors is that consistency beats intensity. It's better to anchor two small tasks every day than to attempt a heroic cleaning sprint that ends in a crash. Choose anchors that feel natural to you and that you can perform the same way on good days and bad days. If you miss an anchor, don't shame yourself. Simply re-connect with the cue the next day. Over time, anchors become part of your mental architecture. They reduce the energy cost of cleaning by turning a needed action into a predictable, almost automatic process. And when your brain encounters a familiar sequence, you are less likely to resist. The power of anchors is their quiet reliability. They don't demand a lot of planning, and they don't require perfect attention. They give you a structure to lean on when motivation is thin and attention is scattered, and they offer a gentle way to sustain progress across days, weeks, and seasons of life. If you're new to anchors, start with one or two that relate to the spaces you use most often. Track what happens when you link a cue to a small action: does the space feel calmer? Do you notice less clutter at the end of the day? Do you feel more in control instead of overwhelmed? Use what you learn to refine the anchors you use, expanding slowly as you gain confidence. Anchors are not a test of willpower; they are a design choice. They let you choose to act in a way that respects your energy and your time, instead of waiting for a mood to arrive that may never come. They invite you to practice a gentle, repeatable routine that makes cleaning a steady part of life rather than a crisis response. And with practice, anchors become automatic, delivering relief with minimal mental effort.

ROTATIONS AND CHECKLISTS TO LIGHTEN THE LOAD

Checklists and rotations are the practical cousins of routines. They are the tools that reduce memory burden and make the next right step obvious. The idea behind rotations is simple: rotate tasks in a way that prevents fatigue from doing the same chore day after day. The brain loves novelty and predictability in equal measure, and rotations give you both. A rotation does not mean you must do everything every day. It means you cycle through tasks so that no single task becomes the entire day's burden. In practice, you can designate a small set of tasks for each day of the week, keeping each day compact and finishable. The key is to schedule only what you can reasonably complete in a short time and to keep the expectations flexible. For instance, on one day you might focus on the kitchen—clearing counters, rinsing dishes, and wiping the sink—while on another day you tackle laundry or mail. The third day could be a quick declutter pass in a living space. You do not need to finish an entire category in one session. You are building a rhythm that allows you to move in and out of tasks with a sense of progress. The concept of a rotation becomes especially powerful when energy fluctuates. On days when you have high energy, you can do longer, more ambitious sessions; on days with low energy, you can lean into the lighter tasks from your rotation. The rotation keeps the workload predictable and prevents the sense of being overwhelmed that tends to accumulate when one busy day turns into several chaotic days. A simple rotation is only part of the equation. You also want a practical checklist you can carry in your pocket or keep on your phone, something that tells you exactly what to do next. The essential idea of a checklist is to reduce memory load by externalizing memory. Instead of recalling a sequence of actions, you consult the list and pick the next item. The critical design principle is to make the checklist minimal, modular, and actionable. Start with a one-page weekly plan that lists four to six tasks and assigns each to a day or a time of day. The wording should be precise and compact. Each item should reveal the next action: clear the counter, start a load, bring items to their homes, sort mail, rinse, dry, fold for laundry, or wipe a surface. The moment you complete an item, you check it off mentally or physically, and you move to the next line. The best checklists are dynamic. They adapt as you learn what works and what doesn't. They are not carved in stone; they are living documents that you update as your energy patterns shift with the seasons, work demands, or family routines. To prevent a checklist from becoming another source of pressure, design it with non-negotiables and optional items. Non-negotiables are the essentials that must get done for your space to function, and you ensure those lines stay accessible and unambiguous. Optional items are where you give yourself the freedom to adjust when energy is tight. If you have an especially draining day, you can skip optional items and still satisfy the core purpose of your checklist. The science behind checklists is straightforward: they reduce decision fatigue and memory load. When you can glance at a single page and see the next action, your brain experiences less friction between intention and action. The human brain wants to be efficient; a well-designed checklist is the shortest path from "I should do something" to "I did something." The rotation and the checklist work together as a system. The rotation determines what you do and when, and the checklist tells you how to do it in the moment. This pairing turns cleaning from a vague ambition into a sequence of tiny, reliable steps. It also creates a feedback loop: as you track your progress, you learn which tasks tend to drain your energy and which require less cognitive overhead. You can then adjust the rotation to place your more demanding tasks on days when you historically perform better, and keep the easier tasks for days when energy dips. A practical way to start is to choose a single space that drives most of your stress, such as the kitchen or the living room, and design a two-week rotation that alternates between a few core tasks. Pair each task with a brief, repeatable action. Then create a one-page checklist for those tasks, with the next action clearly stated. For example, a simple kitchen rotation might look like: Day one address the counters and sink, day two wipe appliances, day three sweep and mop, day four focus on the pantry or fridge for a quick declutter. The exact pattern does not matter as long as it feels feasible and you can stick to it. The checklist should be straightforward: clear the counter, rinse a dish, wipe a surface, bring items to their homes. It should never require you to remember a dozen steps. The less your brain has to juggle, the more likely you are to complete the required actions. It's important to maintain a flexible mindset. If a job takes longer than you expected, adjust. If you wake up in the morning and feel exceptionally drained, you still deserve a plan that allows you to do something useful. Your system should reward progress rather than punish lapses. Over time, your rotations and checklists will become intuitive. You'll learn which cues are most motivating, which tasks tend to stall you, and how to adapt your lists to changing energy levels, schedules, and household dynamics. The ultimate goal is not a flawless sequence but a consistent one. A consistent sequence will produce a quieter home and a steadier mental state, which in turn supports better attention, less decision fatigue, and more opportunities to enjoy the spaces you've created rather than constantly cleaning up after them. As you implement rotations and checklists, you may discover that you naturally skip some items or reorder them based on real-world feedback. That is not failure; it is data. Treat it as information that helps you refine your system to fit your life. Your home should work for you, not the other way around. Rotations and checklists are your invitation to that partnership, a practical compromise between structure and spontaneity that respects the ADHD brain's unique needs while still delivering tangible results.

THE TWO-LEVEL PLAN: NORMAL AND LOW-ENERGY MODES

Two levels, one steady aim. The two-level plan is the backbone of a cleaning system that refuses to abandon you in moments of fatigue or overwhelm. It recognizes that energy, mood, and cognitive load are not constant across the week. Some days you feel capable of a steady routine; other days you need a lighter touch or a scaled-down version of your tasks. The core idea is simple: design a normal plan for high-energy days and a low-energy plan you can switch to when the tank runs dry, without losing your momentum. The normal plan is the one you follow most days. It represents your best effort: a concise set of routines, anchored actions, short rotations, and a clean, clear checklist. It should feel achievable, not aspirational. The low-energy plan is the safety net. It's a smaller, gentler version of your normal plan that you can actually do when fatigue, overwhelm, or disruptions block your usual tempo. The low-energy plan should preserve the integrity of your space while acknowledging that your capacity shifted. You want to avoid a situation where a bad day snowballs into a week-long stall. The two-level plan works because you are always choosing between two viable options. You never reach a point where you tell yourself you must wait until you have courage, energy, or motivation to begin. The choice is pre- baked into your system. On a high-energy day, you follow Plan A. On a low-energy day, Plan B slides into place with minimal friction. The mapping from Plan A to Plan B should be obvious and immediate; you should not need to invent new steps in the middle of a tough day. The design begins with a simple inventory of tasks that keep your space functional. Identify the core routines that underpin your life—kitchen maintenance, laundry flow, mail processing, and a quick weekly reset for spaces that create friction. For each routine, you create two variants: a full version for Plan A and a compact version for Plan B. The full version contains the sequence of steps you would perform if you had ample energy: start a load of laundry, wipe the kitchen counter, sort mail, sweep the floor, and so on. The compact version contains the minimum viable actions that still produce a sense of order: wipe down or rinse, move a handful of items to their proper place, and switch the next required step into a more doable form. When you design Plan B, you want the steps to be tiny and obvious so you can begin immediately. For example, if Plan A for the kitchen is to clear benches, wipe surfaces, load the dishwasher, and sweep, Plan B might be: put away one item that's out of place, run the faucet for a minute to rinse a few dishes, and wipe one surface. The objective of Plan B is not to accomplish less for the sake of avoiding effort; it's to maintain a functioning environment even when energy is scarce. Your two-level plan is also a tool for learning your own patterns. As you track how often you choose Plan B, you gather data about your energy cycles, how long you typically recover, and what kinds of tasks drag you down most. This data becomes the basis for smarter planning in the future. You can incorporate thresholds that automatically trigger Plan B. For example, if you wake up in the morning and feel you can only devote five minutes to a task, your plan automatically switches to Plan B. The automatic switch reduces the friction of decision-making in the moment. And because you have already preemptively mapped Plan B, you don't waste energy debating what to do next. The two-level plan also invites you to experiment with the order of tasks. On high-energy days you might choose to tackle tasks in a deterministic order to maximize impact. On low-energy days, you might choose the simplest, fastest tasks first to build momentum. The key is to preserve a sense of progress, even in tiny increments, so that you don't feel derailed by a rough day. A practical approach to building your two-level plan is to start by listing the essential routines that keep your home functional. For each routine, write down Plan A and Plan B. Then create a set of cues that trigger a switch, such as waking up, returning home, or starting a meal. Finally, implement a simple review ritual, perhaps on Sunday evenings, to adjust your plans based on what happened in the previous week. It's essential that the entire system remains restart-friendly. ADHD brains often need a fresh restart after a setback. The two-level plan supports this by making restarting you twice as easy: you can resume Plan A when energy returns, or you can stay with Plan B until you feel ready to escalate again. The aim is not to push through fatigue at the cost of your well-being. It's to maintain a sense of control through flexible, repeatable options that you can access at a moment's notice. If you can design your system so that the next action is obvious and the energy cost of starting is minimal, you will experience fewer flare-ups of overwhelm and more consistent progress. The two-level plan protects you against the urgent tyranny of the day, giving you a reliable way to respond to changing energy while preserving your long-term goals: a calmer home, a gentler relationship with cleaning, and a sense of competence that scales with your life. It's not about forcing yourself into a single mode; it's about giving yourself a choice that honors your neurodiversity and your humanity. This is the heart of a sustainable ADHD-friendly cleaning operating system: a framework that you can repeat, adapt, restart, and scale, season after season, without shame or burnout.

FOUR
BREAK TASKS DOWN WITHOUT MAKING A 47-STEP LIST

THE SMALLEST POSSIBLE START

When the idea of cleaning or organizing hits your brain, it can feel like you're staring up at a cliff. The sheer height of what needs doing can trigger quick shutdowns, especially if motivation and attention dip at the same moment. The antidote is not willpower or heroic stamina. It's a tiny, almost ridiculous start—the kind you can accomplish in under two minutes. This is the core of what I call the smallest possible start: a next right step so small that your brain can't argue with it, a step that matters enough to move the needle but never so big that it threatens to derail you before you even begin. In ADHD minds, momentum loves small beginnings. A two-minute action is enough to switch the mood from overwhelmed to capable. It's enough to prove to yourself that starting is possible, and once you've started, continuing is more likely than not.

The move is to redefine your tasks as a sequence of small, meaningful micro-actions rather than a long, intimidating list. Think of a minute or two as a gateway, not a ceiling. The phrase you'll want to anchor to is bold and practical: the *next right step*. This is not the next item on a grocery list nor the entire laundry ritual, but the next thing that can be done quickly and clearly, and that nudges the larger goal forward. For example, instead of "tidy the kitchen," your next right step might be "open the dish rack and place the clean, dry dishes in their home," or even more micro: "turn on the sink faucet and rinse the dish that's there." It's not about perfection; it's about moving just enough so that tomorrow feels a little easier.

To choose the right step, scan the environment and ask a few simple questions. What action would reduce visible clutter by the end of two minutes? What can I finish in that window so that it ends with a sense of completion rather than dangling tasks? If a two-minute task feels still too big, ask a deeper but still micro-focused question: could I do this in thirty seconds? The beauty of this approach is that it creates a bridge from motionless inertia to traction. You're not forcing yourself to clean the whole surface; you're asking permission to touch something, to complete a fraction of the work, to prove to your brain that momentum exists.

A typical morning scene can illustrate the method. You walk into the kitchen. A sink full of dishes and a counter with crumbs rise in your perception. The old impulse is to launch into a sprawling plan: "I'll tackle everything on the counter, and then I'll run the dishwasher, then…" That mindset invites resistance because it sounds like a marathon. Instead, pick one micro-step that can be done in under two minutes. Put away one mug. Wipe a small crumb with a damp sponge. Straighten a dish towel, then look again and acknowledge the tiny win. The outcome isn't a perfectly tidy counter; it's a counter that looks and feels a little calmer, which is exactly the air you need to breathe to restart with less shame and more ease tomorrow.

It's worth naming a couple of guardrails that protect this approach from devolving into a scavenger hunt of trivial tasks. First, these steps must matter—there should be a real payoff, such as reducing a source of friction (a heavy pile of mail, a wobbly stack of dishes, a sprouting mess in the sink). Second, they should be simple to start and finish quickly; there's no room for a cascade of tiny decisions that multiply into paralysis. Finally, if you are tempted to drag in a much larger chunk, pivot back to a smaller micro-step. The goal is not to prove you can complete everything in two minutes, but to prove you can start and complete something in two minutes.

The two-minute rule is not a hard limit; it's a mental boundary that lets your brain feel safe enough to begin. If you find yourself in a day where two minutes feels insufficient to make a dent, push the timer to three or five minutes and allow yourself a longer sprint. The key is to stay within a window that you can maintain without mental fatigue spiraling into guilt or shutdown. And remember, you're not abandoning longer tasks. You're simply using a system that tailors itself to how ADHD brains actually work, which is often about frequent, manageable bets rather than heroic, long bets. The essential point is to leave every start with the conviction that you can resume, not that you must perform at peak capacity right away.

As you begin to practice this approach, you'll notice a shift in your relationship with chores. The work no longer lives on a pedestal of shame or a never-ending list. It breathes as a series of small, doable decisions. You train your attention by committing to a micro-action, you train your motivation by rewarding yourself with a visible result, and you train your own body to expect less friction when you begin. The next section will build on this by showing how to make those tiny starts visible across your home through clear, practical zoning. Visualizing progress is one of the most powerful antidotes to ADHD paralysis, and it starts with the smallest possible start.

VISUAL CHUNKING BY AREA

Progress in ADHD-friendly organization often hinges on our brains seeing the finish line, even if only partial. The idea of visual chunking by area turns a sprawling to-do list into a map of approachable zones. Instead of thinking about "the house," you think about "zones" you can complete one by one. The brain is relieved by boundaries, and zones provide them. By dividing a space into smaller, clearly defined patches, you create a sense of accomplishment after each patch is cleaned or organized. The effect is practical: you can see the area change, surface by surface, and the momentum compounds as you move from one zone to the next.

How you choose zones matters as much as how you act within them. Start by walking through your home with a curious eye, not a judgmental one. Notice where clutter gathers and where attention tends to slide. A zone should be small enough that finishing it feels plausible in a single session, yet meaningful enough that finishing it significantly reduces daily friction. A living room might become several zones: a seating zone, a media zone, and a toy or clutter trap zone. A kitchen can partition into the sink zone, the prep zone, and the breakfast bar zone. A hallway might become an entry zone and a mail hook zone. There is no universal blueprint; your zones should reflect your space, your routines, and your unique ADHD pattern.

Once you've drawn a few zones, give each one a simple success criteria. Not every surface needs to be immaculate, but every zone should have a clear, visible state you can recognize as "done for now." The zones become anchors. When you're deciding what to work on, you can point to a single zone as the place to begin, knowing you can complete that zone's set of micro-tasks in one or two sessions rather than returning to the entire space again and again. A zone can be as small as a single countertop with items in their homes or as broad as an entire closet when you choose to tackle it with a plan of attack that respects your energy levels.

Color coding and simple containers reinforce this approach. A color-coded tote or bin for each zone or a set of labeled baskets along a shelf creates a visual signal of what belongs where, and it reduces the mental load of wondering where to place something. When you finish a zone, you don't have to revisit every item in the room to confirm you're done; you need only check that the surfaces within that zone are reasonably clear and that items have a home. The visible progress—before and after photos, a quick glance at the completed zone—fuels motivation and lowers the barrier to starting the next zone.

The zone approach also offers a unique advantage in shared homes. If you live with a partner, roommate, or family member, you can negotiate zones that respect different tolerances and rhythms. You might decide that one person tends to the entry zone while another handles the kitchen zone, with a shared expectation that each zone has a clearly defined "done" state. This reduces the typical friction that arises when people interpret "tidy" differently. With zones, you're not asking for perfection; you're inviting steady, visible progress that you and others can recognize and support.

When a zone feels stuck, bring in a two-minute start to move it forward and then switch to a different zone for a while. The brain loves novelty as long as there's a map to follow. Visual chunking by area gives you that map. It makes the task feel doable because you can see small successes accumulating. It also creates natural breaks that support your energy and focus patterns. In the next section we'll discuss tools that help you start and sustain those zone-focused efforts, including timing methods, the social support of body doubling, and momentum-building tactics that fit ADHD minds at work and at home.

MOMENTUM TOOLS: TIMERS, BODY DOUBLING, AND MOMENTUM

The tendency to stall in the middle of a task, which many ADHD brains recognize all too well, is not a moral failing; it's a signal that the brain is asking for a different kind of support. Momentum is built by tools that lower the friction to start, keep you moving, and then help you pause with a clear path forward. There are several practical tools you can deploy without requiring heroic willpower. Timers create a finite horizon that makes the first move feel safe. When you set a timer for a small window—ten minutes, perhaps, or even five—you invite your brain to commit to a concrete boundary. Within that boundary you don't have to decide again and again whether you should start; you have already decided that you will start and you will stop at the boundary unless you choose to continue. The moment the timer begins, the inertia you've felt begins to bend toward motion. Some days you'll go beyond the timer; on other days, clinging to that boundary is exactly what you need to prevent a meltdown and preserve your energy for later.

Body doubling is another powerful tool. It's not about performing to someone else's standard; it's about sharing the experience of starting. A friend, partner, or even a community group can be there with you in spirit or in person as you embark on a task. The presence of another person—whether you are both in the same room, or you're on a call or video chat—shifts your brain's perception of effort. The moment someone else is there, you're less likely to renege, and more likely to lean into the task long enough to discover that you can finish something. For some people, the most helpful form is a brief check-in at the start: "I'm starting a ten-minute sprint now, want to join for the first five minutes?" For others, it's a longer window where you and your body double share the same micro-goals and hold each other accountable with that light, steady presence.

Momentum tools also include simple rituals and cues that keep you moving. A curated playlist with a steady tempo can synchronize with your pace in a way that feels almost automatic. A specific scent—citrus for alertness, peppermint for focus—paired with a physically easy setup can act as a mental switch that tells your brain, this is the time to begin. A small toolkit placed at arm's reach, containing

BREAK TASKS DOWN WITHOUT MAKING A 47-STEP LIST

a cloth, a spray bottle, and a couple of microfiber towels, reduces the number of decisions you must make to get started. Each time you use these tools, you reinforce the mental pattern that starting is painless and that finishing a micro-task leads to a real outcome.

The choice of which momentum tool to use isn't universal; it's personal. Some days a timer is enough to crack the shell of procrastination; other days, you'll crave the social nudge of body doubling. Some days you'll rely on a crisp playlist, and other days you'll want a quiet, low-stimulation environment. The key is to have a small set of reliable options ready in your toolkit and to practice using them until they feel automatic. Practice is not about becoming a person who never procrastinates; it's about becoming someone who can restart quickly when life interrupts your flow. In practice, you'll try a session with a ten-minute timer and a request for a partner to join you for a five-minute stretch. If that works, you know you've found a rhythm; if it doesn't, you adjust. It's about flexible, restart-friendly strategies rather than rigid, one-size-fits-all routines.

Finally, momentum tools are as much about cognitive comfort as they are about speed. It's not just how fast you act, but how safe you feel taking action. When you combine timers with body doubling and momentum cues, you create a triad of support that tackles the main ADHD obstacles: initiation, sustained effort, and the emotional weight of starting again after a break. You're not trying to outrun your brain's quirks; you're learning to work with them, so your home becomes a reliable space rather than a constant source of stress. In the next section we'll anchor all these methods in a simple, repeatable habit: ending your session with a clear setup step that keeps tomorrow's start friction-free.

END WITH A SETUP STEP

Ending a cleaning or organizing session with a deliberate setup step is a small act, but it protects you from the dreaded restarting hurdle. The setup step is not a grand plan for tomorrow; it's a tiny, practical cue that makes the next start almost inevitable. The logic is simple: you invest a few seconds to remove friction for the next moment you decide to work. This is how you convert a sprint into a reliable routine rather than a sporadic burst of energy followed by a long drought.

A setup step can be as straightforward as arranging the environment so that the next action is obvious and easy. For a kitchen zone, that might mean placing a dish towel and a spray bottle on the counter, with a neat stack of dishware nearby and a clear empty sink. For a clothes closet, it could mean laying out a single garment hanger or setting aside a dedicated bin for the next bag of donations. The precise action matters less than the reduction in decisions that follows. Leaving the area with a single, visible cue makes it natural to pick up where you left off, rather than re-entering a space and wondering where to begin.

Another powerful setup step is to place the exact items you will need for the next step in a ready-to-use container. If you're moving from laundry to folding, place a small basket with clean, dry clothes near the sofa or bed, and include a folding surface and a place to put the folded items. If the next move is paperwork, assemble a simple packet with a folder, a recycle bin for junk, a stamped envelope if mail needs sending, and a pencil for quick notes. The idea is to provide a small, contained kit that travels with you rather than forcing you to hunt for supplies the moment your timer ends. The benefit is simple: you hit the ground running instead of wasting precious minutes gathering tools.

A ready-to-resume state is not just about tools; it's about cadence. You can establish a five-minute wind-down ritual that signals your brain that the work is pausable, not abandoned. In this ritual you identify the exact next step, set out the necessary materials, and decide when you will pause again. If the day ends mid-task, you know exactly how to pick up the next day because the next right step is clearly visible and the setup is intact. For shared spaces, agree on a mutual rule that sets the bar for the end of a session. Perhaps you'll both leave one zone with a visible sign of progress, or you'll rotate who handles the final setup on alternate days. The point is not to achieve perfection at closing time but to minimize the friction that makes restarting feel like a failed reset.

Ultimately, endings that set you up for a smooth restart are a quiet, powerful form of self-respect. They acknowledge that energy and attention fluctuate, and they create a reliable pattern you can lean on as life changes—new job hours, weekend shifts, or caregiving duties. You'll find that when you end with a setup step, tomorrow's start arrives easier, and the days when you slide back into chaos become less common. This chapter has offered you a practical toolkit that respects your brain's rhythm and your home's needs: tiny starts, clear zones, momentum allies, and a thoughtful setup that keeps your home—and your relationship with cleaning—moving forward with kindness and clarity.

FIVE
DECLUTTERING WITH ADHD: KEEP, TOSS, RELOCATE WITHOUT SPIRALING

LIMITS FIRST, LESS CLUTTER

Picture your space as a limited canvas. The container concept asks you to name the boundary before you name the objects. If you were packing a weekend bag, you would choose a fixed size and refuse anything that wouldn't fit. The same logic applies at home. For each category—shirts, desk supplies, kitchen towels—the goal is to decide how much space you will dedicate to it and then keep only what fits there. When your space has a clear limit, debates end before they begin. The ADHD brain can get pulled into endless possibilities and "what ifs." Limits shift that energy back toward action. They turn a looming decision into a quick confirmation: does this item belong in this space, or does it belong somewhere else? With a boundary in place, you gain a compass you can trust even when motivation slips.

The trick is to make the boundary tangible and visible. A single bin, a defined shelf, or a specific drawer becomes the container that holds your decisions. It's not about perfection; it's about a system you can repeat. Start by selecting a real, physical limit you can enforce today. A laundry hamper with a lid. A tote for the entryway. A stackable box that slides under the bed. The exact measurements matter less than the fact that you have a real, boundary-based target. If a category already feels chaotic, reduce it to one container for now, and forgive yourself for not sorting everything all at once.

In practice, limits work best when they're easy to enforce and easy to remember. You can assign a concrete, simple capacity: for example, one tote for seasonal clothing, one bin for accessories, one tray for desk clutter. The key is to avoid tiny, overlapping containers that require constant reshuffling. If a space can hold twenty items, you fill it with your best twenty. If you can't fit a shirt that still feels essential, you either relocate it to a more appropriate space or let go of it with a clear, compassionate rationale. The moment you define how much, you define what matters most in that space, and you reduce the friction of decision-making.

To make this mindset stick, couple it with a practical test. Imagine walking into the space after a two-week break. If the same items would still fit in the container, you've kept the right balance. If not, you have a choice to make: reassess what you count as "essential" or adjust the container size. A larger container might feel freeing for a moment, but it can invite more clutter down the road. A smaller container, chosen deliberately, becomes a signal to prune.

A common entry point is the area that greets you every day. The top of a dresser, the surface of a desk, the seat of a chair. Start there. Decide how much you will allow to reside in that space and what you'll do when it's full. You may decide, for instance, that the desk surface can hold only what you use this week. Anything else either hides away in a properly designated container or goes to another part of the home with a clear timer for revisiting it. The beauty of this approach is in its repeatability. No matter how chaotic a day gets, you can return to that boundary and reset in minutes, not hours.

As you begin applying limits, you'll notice a gentler cadence to decluttering. The decision fatigue eases, because you're not weighing every item against an abstract ideal. You're weighing it against a real, finite space. You're saying, in effect, "This is what this space can hold, and I'll respect that limit." Your ADHD brain experiences this as a map rather than as an endless road of small, daily traps. You get momentum from the first container, and that momentum is your ally in the weeks ahead.

It helps to recognize that limits are not permanent verdicts on your relationship with objects. They're flexible guidelines you can adjust as life changes. If a new hobby fills a corner of your house, you can expand a container or reallocate space. If a different season demands different clothing, you can shift the limits accordingly. The important piece is the rhythm: define the limit, fill with what truly fits, and review with honesty whenever your space feels crowded again. The container concept is not about denying yourself things you love; it's about giving your daily life a reliable frame within which you can function and thrive.

SIMPLE RULES, CLEAR CHOICES

Decision fatigue is a real thing for the ADHD brain. It comes from too many options, too much data, and too little energy to thoughtfully weigh every item. The antidote is simple rules that apply to almost every situation, rules you can remember in a crowded moment and apply with a quick click of your brain. The goal is not to become ruthless—though some days that helper voice will feel like a lifeline—but to establish a practical, repeatable pattern you can trust even when motivation flags.

One of the most powerful rules is the "one pass, one decision" approach. When you sweep a space, you make one pass and make one decision per item: keep, relocate, or toss. You don't do a second pass while you're in the middle of the initial pass. If you pause, you move on. The second pass happens later, when your energy is back. This keeps your mind from circling on the same items all day.

It also mirrors how momentum works in real life: action plus a tiny bit of consistency yields results that compound over days and weeks.

A second rule focuses on usefulness and joy. Utility matters, but so does delight. If an item is useful but dull, it may have to earn its keep by being tucked away neatly in its container and used regularly. If it sparks joy or holds a memory that still matters, it deserves a home where it can be seen or appreciated. If an item pales on both counts, it becomes a candidate for relocation or release. This isn't about object hoarding or emotional neglect; it's about aligning your physical space with your current life and energy, and acknowledging what you actually love enough to maintain.

Third, introduce a soft deadline. Your rules become more real when they have a time anchor. For a desk pile, you might decide to process it within one 15-minute sprint, after which you'll have a few minutes to file, photograph, or relocate the items. The deadline creates a tiny pressure valve that helps your brain move from intention to action without waiting for motivation to magically appear. In practice, you'll begin by applying the rules to a small, manageable area—the top drawer of a desk, a kitchen countertop, a single shelf. The payoff is immediate: a space that looks calmer, a morning routine that starts on a stable note, a sense that you are in charge rather than being overwhelmed by the space around you.

The simplicity of these rules is intentional. ADHD brains crave clear, repeatable patterns rather than long, nuanced decision trees. When you agree to one pass, one decision, one sense of usefulness or joy, you're reducing the mental energy required to stay organized. You're building a habit where the answer to "Should I keep this?" becomes almost automatic because you've trained your reflexes to react to space and utility rather than to fear or guilt. The result is a cleaner space and, more importantly, a calmer mind that knows what belongs where and how it got there.

Over time, these simple rules grow into your personal organizing rhythm. Your energy levels drive how aggressively you apply them, and you'll negotiate the balance between speed and care. Some days you'll move quickly, finishing items in one pass with time to spare. Other days you'll slow down, but you'll still be guided by a consistent approach. The beauty of simple rules is that they scale to your life: a tiny cabinet, a sprawling home, or anything in between. They give you permission to start small, reset often, and keep moving forward without ever blaming yourself for the pace.

To make the rules feel practical, pair them with a quick memory cue. A single keyword or short phrase—Keep, Relocate, Toss—written on a bright post-it above the space, or a caption on your phone wallpaper, can remind you what to do in the moment. The cue acts like a safety net, catching you when fatigue makes choices murky. The aim is to reduce the cognitive load of decision-making, not to erase your humanity or your attachment to your belongings. You are allowed to keep things you love; you are also allowed to move on when your life has moved past certain items. The rules exist to support that flourishing balance.

As you practice, you'll discover a rhythm that matches your energy. On high-energy days you may glide through spaces with quick two-step decisions, finishing tasks before you know it. On lower-energy days you'll still move forward, because the rules remove the burden of endless deliberation. Your home will begin to reflect a consistent pattern: spaces that are clear enough to use, yet flexible enough to accommodate change. The aim is not tidiness for tidiness's sake; it is a home that respects your attention, your time, and your capacity for focus.

STOP THE RELOCATION SHUFFLE

The relocation trap is familiar to many of us. You finish one pile only to discover that another area of the house has become a temporary holding space for "later." The problem isn't laziness or lack of care; it's a cognitive loop that keeps you moving items from one place to another without ever committing to a final destination. You end up with a maze of stacks and a sense that you're making "progress" when in truth you're merely shuffling the same items around with no real end in sight. This is a common pattern in ADHD homes, where the friction of decision-making meets a busy life that makes finishing feels optional.

The antidote is to design a finish line for every item you touch. When you decide to move something, you give it a home with a real address, not a vague "somewhere." A home with a labeled shelf, a specific bin, or a day-by-day schedule. The moment the item has a home, your brain experiences the action as complete rather than provisional. This simple mental switch—finish what you start by giving the item a final home—dramatically reduces the urge to relocate again and again.

Begin with the easiest high-traffic areas, such as your entryway, kitchen counters, and the area around the computer desk. These zones are where your momentum begins and ends each day. Set up micro-systems that force you to close the loop. For example, when you drop something in a filing tray, you promise yourself that you will either file, donate, or relocate the item within the next five minutes, and you set a timer accordingly. If you've spent more than a couple of minutes in that zone without completing the action, you shift your approach: you either create a more straightforward category for that item or you decide to move it to a long-term storage area that you can revisit during a planned weekly declutter.

To prevent the trap long-term, build a simple audits cadence into your routine. At the end of each day, scan the most active spaces and perform one finishing action for anything you touched. It might be as simple as placing a small pile into a labeled box to be sorted during your next "low-energy" session or setting a reminder to complete the action during your next living-space reset. The crucial point is to systematize the finish line. The moment you commit to a home for every item and a deadline for finalizing the placement, you reduce the back-and-forth that steals your energy and your time.

The relocation shuffle thrives on ambiguity. Clarity becomes the antidote. If you can name a final destination for each item before you start moving it, you gain a little bit of control back. Your home stops feeling like a constantly shifting map and starts to feel like a series of stable rooms you can depend on. The goal isn't to enforce a rigid, color-coded universe; it's to create predictable places where things belong so you can find them when you need them and let them go when you don't. With that clarity, you liberate your attention for the tasks that truly matter: the moments of daily living that make your home supportive rather than a source of stress.

A practical test is to observe how a single straight path through a room behaves after you implement the finish-line rule. Do items land on a shelf with a documented function? Do you feel a sense of completion instead of a roll of disorganization in your chest? As you gain confidence, you'll notice a quiet, almost immediate effect: less second-guessing, fewer cycles of shuffling, and a steady improvement in your ability to actually finish routines rather than postponing them.

Remember, the point of stopping the relocation shuffle is not to trap yourself into monotonous routines. It's to create reliable anchors in your space so your brain can relax. When you know where things belong and you've committed to placing them there, you free up energy to use for the things you actually care about—connections, hobbies, rest, and meaningful work. The home becomes a place you can rely on again, rather than a puzzle you must solve every day anew.

SENTIMENTAL CLUTTER, COMPASSIONATE CARE

Sentimental items carry a different kind of weight. They can be beautiful reminders of people, moments, and stages of life, but they can also become emotional anchors that prevent you from moving forward. For many of us with ADHD, guilt compounds the difficulty: am I allowed to let go of this object when it still holds value? Is a memory less real if it's not physically preserved? The answer, in one word, is compassion. You deserve a space that functions for your life now, and memories deserve a respectful handling that honors their value without letting them hijack your daily living.

Compassion starts with boundaries that protect your energy while still honoring what matters. Set a maximum amount of sentimental items you'll keep in a given space and decide what you'll do with the rest. The limit is not a dismissal; it's a way to create space for what you actively use, love, and need to feel safe in your home. The moment a memory object becomes a burden rather than a bridge to the past, you deserve to adjust, not punish yourself for feeling that way. Your love for a memory does not require you to carry the physical object everywhere you go. In many cases, a photograph, a story, or a voice recording can preserve the essence without the full weight of the original item.

The next step is to design safe, compassionate storage strategies that honor the sentimental value while making the memory accessible when you want it. A shadow box that houses a few selected mementos can serve as a weekly ritual. A memory shelf can showcase a rotating collection of photos or tokens that you refresh six times a year. For documents and letters, a simple box labeled with dates or people keeps the material organized without drowning you in a river of paper long after the moment has passed.

Digital alternatives can dramatically ease the burden of physical items. Take photos of keepsakes or scan documents and then store the digital copies in a well-organized cloud album or drive. A digital archive can be searchable, easy to back up, and much smaller than the original object collection. You are not required to "capture every memory" in physical form to honor it. You're allowed to choose a smaller, more sustainable footprint that still allows you to revisit your memories without becoming overwhelmed by the archival project.

When you do decide to release an item, do so with intention. Writing a short note to yourself or to the memory can provide closure. You might say, "I'm grateful for the moment this item represented, and I'm choosing to pass it on so someone else can create new memories with it." If you're releasing it into donation or recycling, you can add a brief line to your note about where it will go or who could benefit. This simple ritual reframes letting go as an act of care rather than a loss, which can soften the emotional edge that often accompanies sentimental decluttering.

If you're unsure whether an item belongs in the keep pile, use a compassionate tiebreaker. Put it in a small, clearly labeled box marked 'Maybe Later.' Schedule a quick revisit in a month or two. If you haven't looked at the item during that window, it's a strong signal you can release it with kindness. This approach protects you from impulsive attachments while still honoring the value of memories that matter.

Ultimately, the heart of compassionate sentimental decluttering is this: you deserve a home that supports your best self today, even as you carry forward the memories that shaped you. You can hold onto what truly adds meaning while letting go of the rest with gentleness and respect. Your environment should reflect your present life, not be a white-knuckled museum of the past. By setting compassionate limits, choosing practical storage, and embracing gentle releasing rituals, you can live with memories without letting them trip you up. The goal is a home that makes room for living, growing, and continuing to love the people and moments that have shaped you, without adding a daily burden that blocks your progress.

SIX
LAUNDRY THAT DOESN'T TAKE OVER YOUR LIFE

SIMPLIFY THE WARDROBE AND SUPPLIES

When laundry feels like a whack-a-mole game, it's usually because there are too many moving parts fighting for attention. The wardrobe swells with items you never wear, clothes that don't fit the life you actually live, and essentials that get buried under a mountain of "almosts." In ADHD terms, every unnecessary decision creates friction at a moment when you already have limited motivation. The goal of simplifying isn't to turn your closet into a museum of perfect outfits. It's to reduce the number of decisions you have to make every day so you can actually get laundry to behave instead of delegating chaos to happen again tomorrow.

A compact wardrobe is not a prison; it is a runway for calm. Think of a capsule of garments that covers your core needs without duplications. The idea isn't to chase a perfect capsule but to tune your closet until a typical outfit selection feels almost automatic. A practical starting point is to reduce to items you actually wear in the season and in your everyday life. If you reach for the same handful of shirts week after week, you probably don't need eight nearly identical options in your drawer. If you never reach for a pair of jeans that live at the back of the closet, it's time to rehome them. The aim is fewer choices, not fewer outfits. A leaner wardrobe lowers decision fatigue, which in turn lowers the craving to postpone laundry because the pile feels bigger than the closet you're trying to fill.

As you trim, give yourself permission to learn as you go. The next right step isn't about a perfect verdict today; it's about a more usable closet tomorrow. Decide on a rough cap for how many tops, bottoms, and layers you'll keep. You don't have to nail exact numbers. You do want to notice patterns: items you always wear, items you wear only in certain weather, things that have lost elasticity or shape, pieces you love but can't fit into your current routine. If you're unsure, try this simple, ADHD-friendly yardstick: if you haven't worn it in three months and there isn't a viable reason you'll reach for it soon, consider letting it move on. You can test this with a "two-tie" rule—keep a piece if you can imagine pairing it with at least two other items in your daily life. If not, it's time to thank it for serving and set it free.

When it comes to the wardrobe, materials matter as much as style. Breathable fabrics that don't require delicate handling cut down the mental load. If you dislike ironing or special care, lean toward fabrics that hold up with gentle care and air-drying. Lightweight options can still feel presentable and versatile, which reduces the pressure to keep a large variety of outfits on standby for every possible occasion. The point is to minimize complexity without sacrificing a sense of personal style. If you know you dislike certain textures or fabrics, don't force them into your life just because they look good on a hanger. Your closet should be an ally, not a trapdoor.

Alongside your clothes, simplify supplies that touch your laundry process. A single, sturdy hamper system is enough for most households. One hamper in the bedroom for dirty clothes is simple and reduces the urge to carry laundry across the house repeatedly. A dedicated laundry kit near the machine—consisting of one detergent, one stain remover, and a small bottle of fabric softener if you use it—removes the decision fatigue of hunting for supplies mid-load. If space is tight, a compact three-in-one bottle can cover several needs and stay out of the way. The fewer bottles you have to juggle, the less you have to think about when you're ready to start a load.

Labeling can help without feeling like a science project. A simple system uses plain tags with words or pictures where there's a real standard workflow. For example, a small tag on the inner lid of the washer can remind you that this cycle suits everyday clothing, while a tag on the dryer handles towels and linens. The labels don't need to be fancy; they just need to guide you back to the same routine when fatigue or distraction creep in. The idea is consistency, not perfection. A predictable routine—where you know exactly where the clothes go, what detergent to use, and how long a cycle typically runs—creates a mental map you can rely on on an ADHD brain day.

As you implement simplifications, observe what happens to your momentum. Do you find yourself more willing to start a load in the morning because the decision is obvious? Do you notice fewer trips back to the closet to pull the wrong items? When you remove the friction that comes with choice overload, you create space for momentum to build. A lighter wardrobe is not about a bare life; it's about a life where laundry takes up a smaller footprint in your brain and in your home.

If you have a partner or a shared living situation, use these simplifications as a shared contract rather than a unilateral rule. Sit down and agree on a joint minimum viable wardrobe, a shared set of laundry supplies, and a common place for the laundry kit. The goal is to reduce conflict that stems from competing standards and different energy levels. A clear, mutually accepted plan reduces the need for lecture or blame when the pile grows. You're not asking anyone to rigidly conform; you're crafting a system that respects diverse routines and keeps the home moving forward even when one person is on a higher energy day than another.

Ultimately, simplifying the wardrobe and supplies is about turning laundry from a runaway train into a gentle hum. The less there is to decide, the easier it becomes to take the next step—and the next one after that. You want a system that feels boring in all the right ways: predictable, repeatable, and forgiving enough to work even when you forget a load or neglect folding for a week. The goal isn't to eliminate laundry's presence from your life. It's to reduce the emotional charge around it, so you can address it with calm, steady action instead of fear and shame.

BASKETS, ZONES, AND FLOW

A home where laundry doesn't own you starts with a simple map: zones that mirror your movement through a day and a household. In ADHD-friendly terms, you want to reduce the distance between action and result. The further your laundry has to travel to be sorted, started, and stored, the higher the likelihood you'll stall somewhere along the way. The solution is not a grand redesign but small, consistent adjustments that keep clothes landing where they belong rather than piling up in places that make you feel overwhelmed.

Think of three zones that matter most: a dirty clothes zone near each bedroom, a sorting zone near the laundry machine, and a storage or folding zone near where you live. The dirty clothes zone serves as a sink for the day's wear, a place that catches towels and socks before they drift into other rooms. The sorting zone is where clothes move from the hamper into their destiny—wash, dry, or hang. The storage zone is where the finished articles land, ready to be worn or put away. The aim is to create a flow that feels almost automatic, so you don't have to drag your thinking through every step every time.

To keep this flow intact, give each zone a clear, visible home. A basket or bin can act as a magnet, pulling clothes toward the right destination. In a compact setup, you might keep a single roller cart with three bins parked at the foot of the bed, one bin for dirty clothes collecting by the nightstand, one for items headed for wash, and one for items that can go straight to the dryer or closet if you're sure they're ready for wear. If you're in a larger space, it can be as simple as placing a laundry hamper near the door to the bedroom, a labeled sorting tray in the laundry area, and a dedicated shelf or bin for finished clothes near the closet. The key is that the items land where they should with minimal carrying and minimal decision-making.

Labels matter, but they don't have to be elaborate. A few simple words or gentle icons can guide action when fatigue makes decision-making hard. For instance, a tag that reads Dirty near the bedroom corner clearly signals where clothes should go, while a tag above the machine signals what goes where after washing. The labels don't have to be permanent or fancy; they just need to be legible and aligned with how your home actually moves clothes on a daily basis.

The flow should respect the rhythm of your life. On busy days, you want the laundry to be forgiving enough that you can start a load in the evening without firing up a rescue mission. On slower days, you want the same system to be capable of handling extra items without spiraling into backlog. That means leaving some space in each zone for a few items you're not sure about—clothes that you're not ready to decide on or that you're saving for a weather shift. The zones aren't a rigid map; they're a safety net that keeps laundry from turning into a scavenger hunt every time you walk through the room.

If you share a living space, you'll want to co-create zones with your housemates or partner. A shared apartment can benefit from a communal sorting area and a clear set of expectations about where to place clothes that are clean and where to place items that need to be rewashed. It's not about policing each other; it's about agreeing on a cadence that respects different routines and energies. A simple, practical approach is to designate a central laundry zone that everyone can access, and offer a quick daily check-in to adjust the flow as life changes. When everyone has a stake in the flow, the system feels fair and doable rather than punitive.

The beauty of a well-designed flow is that it becomes almost invisible. You don't need willpower to run it; you simply need to pause long enough to put items in the right zone and then let the machine and the closet do the rest. The ADHD brain thrives when friction is minimized, and the zones and flow design are all about friction reduction. When clothes go where they belong without argument, you gain clarity and momentum. Small, consistent wins ripple outward, reducing anxiety about laundry and freeing up cognitive space for other tasks that truly require your attention.

There will be days when a load is forgotten or a pile grows larger than the zones can handle. That's not failure; it's information. The aim is to notice where the flow breaks and to adjust the zones or the labels so that the next attempt feels easier. The laundry map is flexible by design, and its value lies in how quickly you recover from a hiccup. The more you practice recognizing when to realign zones, the steadier your routine becomes. As with all ADHD-friendly systems, the goal is not to be perfect but to have a system that works well enough most days, so you can keep moving forward instead of spiraling backward.

FOLDING ALTERNATIVES

Folding is one of those areas that can trigger a lot of inner resistance. For some people, folding is a tiny ritual that signals the completion of a load and creates a neat, tidy drawer. For others, folding feels like a chore that amplifies the sense that laundry is a never-ending story. The truth is that there isn't a universal rule about folding, only choices that fit your energy, space, and preferences. ADHD-friendly living invites you to choose methods that you can maintain without turning laundry into a moral test.

Let's normalize folding as a choice rather than a requirement. If you genuinely enjoy folding and it helps you stay organized, keep it in your routine. If you dread it but still want a sense of order, consider folding substitutes that give you the look you want with less mental energy. Hanging clothes directly after washing saves folding time for some people, while others find that rolling and stacking items in drawers achieves the same effect without the dreaded crease chase. The critical piece is to decide what you'll actually do, then set up your environment to support that decision.

One approach is to design a "fold when you must" system. This could mean you fold only certain items that tend to wrinkle or need to be hung immediately, such as shirts and dresses, while keeping towels and casual wear on a simple roll-and-stack method. A second option is to embrace hang-drying while clothes are still damp enough to prevent wrinkles, then finish the process by hanging or folding when you have more energy. A third option is the minimalist route: skip folding altogether for a subset of items and keep them in a tidy bin or on a shelf where you can easily grab without unfolding every piece. If space is tight, you might store rolled clothes in drawers or shelves in a way that allows you to see what you have at a glance.

Whatever folding method you pick, the goal is consistency rather than complexity. A predictable approach reduces the load on your memory. A "good enough" fold is better than a perfect fold that never happens. You are aiming for a system you can sustain even when you're tired, distracted, or pressed for time. If you see a shirt you love and notice it's wrinkled, that's not a failure. It's a cue to adjust the system in a small way so future loads go smoother.

For caregivers and households with multiple people, folding preferences can become a pain point if they aren't aligned. The key is to agree on a standard that suits the largest number of people involved and to keep the rules lightweight. A simple rule can be enough: shirts go on hangers or bins ready for use; socks and undergarments live in properly labeled drawers or bins; and towels live in a separate shelf or bin. When the rule is straightforward, it's easier for everyone to participate without conflict.

If you're experimenting with a new folding or storage method, give yourself a trial period. Try it for two weeks and observe how much you actually use it and how much stress it removes. ADHD brains respond to feedback quickly when they can see a visible win. If the new method creates optimism and less resistance, keep it. If not, revise. The objective isn't to conform to someone else's ideal but to land on a routine that feels reliable and less exhausting for you, in this place and this season of life.

Another practical consideration is how clothing is displayed and reached for. In a small space, rolling clothes and stacking them in a shallow bin or drawer can make it easier to see what you have at a glance. The cognitive load of searching for a particular item becomes a non-issue when you can pull out a single neatly arranged stack rather than wading through a pile. If you prefer the look of folded stacks, you can still achieve that effect with rolled or subdivided storage. The main idea is to avoid the mental burden of digging through disorganized piles each morning.

In practice, the best folding approach is the one you don't hate doing. It's about creating an organization that invites you to reuse it rather than dread it. If you can say, with sincerity, that you enjoy a particular method or at least don't dread it, you'll be more likely to keep the routine over time. That is transformative in ADHD living: small changes that you can actually stick with accumulate into a big difference over weeks and months.

If you share space with others, discuss folding expectations with kindness and clarity. The goal isn't to force a single method upon everyone but to identify how each person can participate in a shared system. A practical approach is to choose a primary method that works for the majority and designate exceptions for the people who struggle with the chosen method. The important thing is to maintain a sense of teamwork and a shared end goal: a laundry routine that doesn't dominate your life but supports your daily living with less drama and more dignity.

THE LAUNDRY RECOVERY PLAN

Backlogs happen. You're human, and laundry is not the measure of your worth. The real question is how quickly you can reset after a stretch when the pile got away from you. A recovery plan is not a guilt trip; it's a practical, hopeful path back to a manageable routine. It starts with recognizing the moment you're in: the backlog exists, and you have capacity in you to reduce it through small, repeatable actions. The recovery plan is built around two principles ADHD brains respond to well: short, visible wins and flexibility to restart when life shifts. The aim is to move from a crisis mindset—where every load feels like a deadline—to a steady loop that you can sustain, even on bad days.

Begin with a quick assessment. Look at what's accumulated: a pile of clean clothes to be folded, towels that need a quick run, and a trunk of items that have become a backlog in the laundry cycle. Acknowledge the backlog without judgment and create a plan that respects your current energy level. The plan should begin with the easiest, least intimidating steps. If the sight of a large pile makes you want to walk away, break the task into microchunks: collect two baskets of dirty clothes, start one small load, and set a timer for a short interval. Short intervals feel manageable; they create a sense of momentum rather than mounting pressure. The moment you complete a small goal, celebrate the tiny victory. It might be the clink of the washing machine drum starting, a loaded tote of clean clothes sliding into a shelf, or the sight of a folded stack that looks neat enough to grab on the way out the door.

A practical recovery rhythm can look like this: designate a specific, realistic time block for a backlog reset, and treat it as a non-negotiable appointment with yourself. You begin by gathering the current dirty clothes into a single, manageable collection point. You start a wash with the items that are easiest to wash and most likely to dry quickly. You allow yourself a brief moment to destress, then you move a second small load into the machine. If you can, you splash a little energy into folding or hanging just enough clothes to restore the sense that your space is reclaiming order. The point is not to empty the entire backlog in one sit-down; it's to chip away at it in a way that respects your energy patterns and your real life.

The next right step is always the smallest one that makes the most difference. If the room is chaotic, your next right step might be to create a mini landing zone in a corner—one hamper, one folding tray, one small shelf that can hold a handful of neatly folded items. If you're in a steady flow, your next right step may be to sort a recently laundered batch, place it in its destined drawer, and start a fresh load. The emphasis is on reducing friction, not on achieving a magazine-worthy outcome in a single day.

A common ADHD pitfall is letting a backlog escalate into a self-fulfilling story of "I'll never get ahead." To guard against that, turn the backlog into a tracking sheet of small wins. You don't need a fancy system; a simple list or a visual board where you can move a card from "to wash" to "done" can be enough to show progress. The physical act of moving a card, seeing the line shift from one column to another, provides a cue that you have regained control. The board acts like a mirror of your momentum, not a scoreboard that measures your worth.

The recovery plan also accounts for real life. It isn't a plan for a perfect world; it's a plan for a life that changes day to day. On days when energy is too low for any meaningful folding, you can still create a small victory by simply loading the washing machine and pressing start. On days when you've got a surprising surge of momentum, you can push a bit further and complete a more substantial set of tasks, like sorting a pile and placing finished items away. The idea is to ride the wave of the day rather than fighting against it.

Finally, use the recovery plan to inform future practice. If you notice that you frequently miss loads because you forget to start the machine, find a cue that fits your routine. It could be a reminder placed on the bathroom mirror, a phone alert timed with when you wake up, or a habit that a friend or partner can help you initiate each day. If you notice a recurring friction point—like a stubborn backlog on towels or linens—adjust your plan to give those items a dedicated, fixed place in the flow. Your system should adapt to your life and not the other way around. The best laundry system for ADHD is the one that keeps evolving with your energy levels, your schedule, and your tolerance for structure.

As you work your way through the recovery process, you'll feel a change in your relationship with laundry. It will become less about a crisis you must conquer and more about a predictable loop you can ride. You'll discover that you can reset after a tough day, and you can start again tomorrow with a plan that respects your brain and your home. The real victory is not the elimination of every wrinkle or every sock that escapes a drawer. The real victory is a home that supports you in small, doable steps and a life that lets you breathe a little easier, even when the laundry basket sits nearby.

SEVEN
KITCHEN AND DISHES: FROM DOOM PILES TO DAILY USABILITY

DISH MINIMUMS AND BACKUP PLANS

Dishes have a gravity all their own in a home run by an ADHD rhythm. It's not the thrill of a new organizing method that grabs you; it's the silent dread of the sink piling up and the moment you realize you're washing yesterday's bowls while you cook today's dinner. The idea of dish minimums is simple and deeply practical: decide ahead how many dishes you actually need for a typical day, and then decide what counts as an acceptable backup. Rather than chasing an immaculate kitchen, you're building a tiny system that keeps you functional and reduces the energy drain of a looming sink avalanche. For many adults with ADHD, the goal is not perfection but predictability, a small set of rules that apply every day, even when motivation dips or time vanishes in a blink.

Start with a core set that feels doable, not overwhelming. A practical baseline for one or two people might be two dinner plates, two bowls, two mugs, two forks, two spoons, and two knives. Add a couple of cooking utensils you actually reach for, and you're close to a complete daily cycle. The idea is to have enough so you can eat a few meals without washing in the middle of the next one, without feeling you're permanently living inside a dishwashing nightmare. The numbers aren't sacred. They should match your eating patterns, your energy levels, and your tolerance for rearranging dishware after a busy day. If your usual pattern is to eat cold leftovers or simple meals, you'll naturally get by with fewer items. If you love cooking and entertain often, you'll want more. The trick is to set a baseline you can sustain even when fatigue lands or when you forget a cycle and your sink becomes a magnet for gravity and guilt alike.

Backup options exist for the inevitable days when you simply cannot keep up. Paper plates and disposable utensils can be a lifeline for nights when you're bone-tired and the energy isn't there for any washing at all. They don't have to be a default, but they can be a conscious, planned part of your system. The key is to decide, in advance, how and when you'll use them. If you opt to keep a small stash of paper plates, keep them in a clearly labeled bin or cabinet near where you store the dishware so you don't have to hunt for them when you're already depleted. When you accept that backups exist, you flip the script from shame into strategy. You're not trying to prove you're perfect; you're building space for life as it actually happens, including days when you're running on fumes.

In practice, this means designing a kitchen where the minimum set stays clean more often than not, and the backup options are easy to access without adding extra friction. Consider placing the core dishware in an ordinary routine—dishes go from the table to the dishwasher or sink to be cleaned, then back into their shelves in a predictable rotation. The backup stash sits in a separate, easily reachable place, perhaps in a low cabinet near the dishwasher or a small bin under the sink. The key is that you know exactly where to go when you need it, and you know that using backups is a choice you make, not a crisis you stumble into.

If you're sharing a home, the dish minimums become a joint agreement rather than a personal concession. Sit with a partner or a roommate and decide on a shared baseline—how many place settings you'll keep, how many backup sets you'll allow, and how you'll guard against the sink becoming a pressure cooker. This conversation isn't about policing each other; it's about removing the friction that comes from misaligned expectations. The discipline of a shared baseline reduces daily arguments and makes it possible to restart after a rough stretch without shame or blame. When someone forgets, the structure remains intact, and the household can return to its rhythm without the emotional wreckage that often accompanies clutter.

To make the system resilient, anchor reminders to real-life cues. A small timer or a note by the sink can remind you to: assess the dish situation, decide whether you're washing or swapping in backups, and then complete the chosen action. The cue matters more than the exact action; the aim is to reduce the gap between intention and behavior. You don't need a perfectly clean sink to have a good day; you need a plan that allows you to salvage control when you wake up on a chaos morning.

In the end, dish minimums and backups aren't about denying yourself comfort or convenience. They're about structuring a lean, forgiving routine that reduces what ADHD tends to amplify: procrastination, guilt, and the sense that a single misstep will ruin the week. You deserve a kitchen that serves you, not one that serves fear. Start with a small, honest baseline, add your backups as a deliberate choice, and watch how this quiet system shifts how you feel about meals, cooking, and the after-dish routine. The result is not a spotless kitchen but a reliable one—one that supports you through the busy days and gives you space to restart tomorrow without a perfect yesterday to anchor your mood.

As you begin to implement the dish minimum approach, you'll notice a subtle but important shift. Your sink no longer yawns at you from across the room with an overwhelming gravity. Instead, it sits there as a controlled endpoint of a routine you can predict. You'll be able to choose meals with less mental load, knowing that at the end of the day you can finish with a clean, usable kitchen rather than a looming pile of undone tasks. And when the day calls for backups, you won't panic; you'll reach for the paper plates with a calm, practiced ease. This is the everyday magic of a practical baseline: it makes a home that functions even on days when you don't feel like starring in a cleaning montage.

COUNTERTOP RULES THAT STICK

Surfaces have a way of mirroring our mental state, especially when ADHD makes decision fatigue feel like a constant invitation to drift. Countertops are not just surfaces; they are friction points where the day either flows or grinds to a halt. The core idea behind countertop rules is simple: define what belongs there, and enforce a short, repeatable cleanup that happens every day. When you keep the right items out of sight or in designated places, you reduce the amount of friction between you and a functioning kitchen. The result is a space that supports you rather than taxes your attention. You'll learn to define what is allowed on the counters so they don't become a catch-all for mail, gadgets, keys, and other life's detritus that never seems to find a home.

Begin by creating a single, clear rule: only items that have a daily, finished-use purpose can occupy the countertop. This means a bowl or tray for mail that you'll sort within the day, a small jar for a few essential cooking tools that you actually use, and perhaps a coffee station that remains aesthetically organized and free of clutter. Everything else should have a defined home elsewhere. The rule sounds almost too simple to matter, but it acts as a mental gatekeeper. With ADHD, many surfaces become friction magnets. A single rule reduces the decision-making load: you don't have to decide what to do with every piece of clutter in the moment—you only need to check if it belongs on the counter right now.

To make this rule stick, you need a practical, inviting process for the items that do belong there. Consider a small, dedicated tray near the entrance to the kitchen or near your typical landing spot after shopping. This tray collects items that truly need quick attention, like a grocery list, a receipt you'll process later, or a volunteer key for a shared space. The rest of the mail or gadgets belongs in a designated bin, drawer, or shelf. The tray helps you sleep on a better system by making the intentional choice to place items there rather than scattering them across the counter and into your cognitive blind spots.

Another crucial component is the "one in, one out" philosophy for counter items. Every item that makes it to the surface should have a plan for leaving the surface within a fixed window—ideally by the end of the day. This doesn't require perfect tracking; it simply asks you to decide, before you touch the surface, what will happen to that item after you finish using it. If you have mail on the counter, decide when you'll open and sort it and when you'll file or discard it. If you have a gadget on the counter, decide whether it's going back into its box, into a charging station, or into a drawer. The trick is to translate intention into a tiny, doable action that you can complete today, regardless of your energy level.

Visibility is also a powerful ally. The less you can see of unwelcome clutter, the less it crowds your attention. Use discreet storage that still feels accessible. A shallow bin under the sink for gadgets you rarely use, or a camouflaged basket tucked in a corner can make a big difference. If you can't resist certain items that always end up on the counter—like your car keys, a lamp, or a charging cable—find a single, dedicated station for each item and keep it neatly arranged. The aim is not to pretend clutter doesn't exist but to recognize that a large amount of it on the counter invites 90-second decision cycles that exhaust you. A well-defined surface, with limited, purposeful items and a clear routine for upkeep, gives your brain more room to focus on what matters.

On days when you're operating with limited energy, the rule protects you from the drift into chaos. It's easier to place items where they belong when you know there is a predictable "end of day" action. A quick reset becomes a ritual you can perform in a single breath: check what's on the counter, determine if it has a home, and make a single, intentional move to return it there. If you're cohabitating with others, these rules can extend into shared spaces through quick, compassionate dialogue about what belongs on counters and what doesn't. You're not policing the home; you're making space for a routine that reduces friction and respects the realities of ADHD.

The payoff is subtle and cumulative. Countertops that stay relatively clear reduce the mental load you carry when you cook, clean, or prepare for guests. You'll find that you can see more clearly what needs to be done, and the actions you take feel easier because they aren't fighting against a wall of competing items. The goal is not to achieve sterile perfection but to maintain a calm, usable space that makes daily tasks doable, even on days when motivation is scarce. When you see the countertop as a tool rather than a threat, you'll make it a habit to keep it in a state that supports your day rather than sabotages it.

As with the dish-minimum system, consistency matters more than intensity. Set a three-minute rule: if you're about to sit down or start a meal, quick-scan the counters and determine if anything needs to be cleared away or moved. Then perform one focused action—return a stray item to its home, wipe a small surface with a damp cloth, or store a gadget in its charger. Repetition creates reliability, and reliability is what ADHD brains need to feel confident in their environment. You don't have to love tidying to benefit from this approach; you only have to choose small, repeatable actions that you can actually perform when energy is high or low. The countertop rules that stick are not a grand plan; they are a set of gentle, repeatable nudges toward a space you can trust to support your day.

FRIDGE AND PANTRY WITHOUT OVER-ORGANIZING

The fridge and pantry can feel like corporate storage rooms when you're trying to manage ADHD. The goal is not to create a perfect, unapproachable system but to design simple categories and a layout that makes sense in a real, busy kitchen. When you allow yourself to keep things visible and reachable rather than perfectly sorted, you're more likely to use what you have, reduce waste, and avoid the emotional drain of endless reorganizing. The most sustainable fridges and pantries are not the ones that look pristine; they are the ones that are easy to navigate, easy to inventory, and forgiving when life gets loud.

A practical rule of thumb is to keep the fridge organized into a small number of broad categories, and to keep the pantry similarly streamlined. Think three broad groups for the fridge: everyday staples that you reach for most often, items to consume soon, and items you can freeze or repurpose into future meals. The pantry can be arranged around weekly needs: proteins, grains and starches, and snacks or quick meals. The beauty of this approach is that you aren't forced into elaborate labeling schemes or time-consuming reorganizations. You just create space for what's likely to be used and make the path to use obvious rather than hidden.

Visibility is your friend here. In the fridge, store the essentials at eye level and within easy reach. Place produce in clear bins so you can see what needs to be used first. Group dairy, condiments, and leftovers in a way that you can scan at a glance. If you love roasted vegetables, keep them in a shallow container that you can lift straight onto the counter for a quick meal base. The goal is to reduce the cognitive load required to decide what to cook with what's available. If you must rummage deeper into the fridge to find what you need, you're likely to abandon the search and default to takeout or a less healthful option. By keeping items at arm's reach and clearly grouped, you shift cooking from a scavenger hunt to a straightforward choice.

In the pantry, use simple zones rather than rigid shelves. A grab-and-go zone holds items you rely on for quick meals or busy mornings. A rotation zone helps you watch expiration dates with minimal effort. A bulk or bulk-ish zone keeps mass staples within reach, but not so cluttered that you can't see what's inside. The overarching principle is that you want to be able to locate and use what you have without a mental tax. If a jar has moved to the back of a shelf and stays there for weeks, it's not a successful organization; it's a reminder that the system isn't working for you.

A key element is the idea of not over-organizing. ADHD brains often freeze when asked to maintain a perfect system that requires constant upkeep. Simplicity is the antidote. Containers that are the same size can stack neatly and be labeled quickly with a marker, or you can use a simple color-coded approach if color helps you remember where things go. The aim is to reduce the number of categories you need to track. If you're never going to sort through 15 different herbs, don't pretend you will. Choose a handful of items you actually use and keep them easy to see and access. When you do buy new items, consider how they fit into your three-category approach rather than jamming them into a crowded space.

The practical benefits are immediate. You'll waste less food because you can quickly identify what needs to be used soon and what can be frozen. You'll avoid the stress of a refrigerator that feels like a black hole, where you recall nothing and lose track of leftovers. You'll cook more with what you have, which reduces mental load and can improve mood and motivation. And if you share your kitchen, you'll find it easier to align with others when the system is simple and obvious. The most important factor is that the pantry and fridge stay usable without becoming a chore in themselves. If something feels hard to maintain, you've probably added too much structure. Scale back, keep it visible, and let the space support your day rather than demand perfection from it.

To close this section with a practical vision: imagine opening the fridge to see clearly labeled, accessible compartments with a weekly plan on the door. Produce sits in transparent bins at eye level, dairy items near the back wall for quick checks, leftovers neatly stacked in shallow containers, and a reminder to use items from the soon-to-expire zone before they go bad. In the pantry, imagine three shelves that make sense at a glance: a "fast meals" zone with pasta, rice, and sauces; a "protein and staples" zone with canned beans, tuna, and soups; and a "snacks and extras" zone that keeps things you actually reach for without hunting. The goal is a space that invites use, not a space that punishes you for not keeping it pristine. If you approach your fridge and pantry with three simple categories and a commitment to visibility, you'll notice a remarkable drop in food waste, decision fatigue, and the energy required to stock and maintain your kitchen.

The endgame of fridges and pantries that aren't over-organized is a daily sense of agency. You can plan a week's meals with less mental gymnastics, you can swap items with confidence, and you can rest easy knowing you'll not lose track of what you have. A simplified system offers flexibility for changing seasons of life, for shared kitchens, and for the moments when you just can't stand another reorganizing sprint. This is not about having everything perfectly labeled; it's about having enough clarity to cook and nourish yourself with fewer detours and less stress. When your fridge and pantry support you in real life, you're not chasing magic; you're embracing practicality. And that practical alignment is where sustainable habit begins to grow.

A final note: backups and simplifications must be sustainable. If you find a technique works for a week and then becomes a burden, it's not a system—it's a fad your ADHD brain is unlikely to sustain. Revisit your categories, adjust the placement of items, and let the space evolve with you. You deserve a kitchen where food becomes nourishment rather than a daily struggle.

With a fridge that helps you see what you have and a pantry that makes cooking possible, you'll notice a shift in how you plan meals, how you shop, and how quickly you can respond to the daily demands of life. The goal is to create a space that reduces friction, not one that creates it. When your food storage feels calm and predictable, your meals will feel lighter, your decisions easier, and your energy more available for the rest of your day.

QUICK CLEAN ROUTINES THAT STICK

The daily chore cycle doesn't have to feel like a personal indictment. For many people with ADHD, a short, repeatable routine after meals is what turns a potential crisis into a manageable moment. Quick clean routines are not about spending hours cleaning; they're about finishing the task you started in a few focused minutes, then letting your day move forward. The aim is to create a post-meal rhythm that yes, happens, even when you're tired, overwhelmed, or distracted. You want a routine that you can initiate with the smallest possible friction, and then complete with a sense of forward momentum. This is where tiny habits become mighty: a few deliberate actions that accumulate into a calmer kitchen and a less chaotic mind.

A practical first step is the simplest: after you finish your meal, take intentional action that resets the area. This could mean clearing the dining surface and loading it into the dishwasher or hand-washing only the items that won't fit, then wiping the table and the edges of the counters. You don't need to scour every inch; you only need to perform the one thing that prevents the day from turning into an endless pile. The rhythm should be almost automatic, something you can do with your eyes half-closed on a low-energy day, and something you can spice up on a high-energy day by expanding a little further to put away containers or sweep a light trail of crumbs. The moment you complete this small action, you've achieved a clean, usable space that invites you to keep going or to rest with a clear conscience.

A timer can be your ally here, but not a tyrant. Use it to create a sense of urgency that's gentle rather than paralyzing. Set a short interval of two to five minutes for a

KITCHEN AND DISHES: FROM DOOM PILES TO DAILY U... 99

focused reset. In those minutes you can wipe surfaces, return dishes to their proper places, and pre-stage the next meal's setup if you'll be cooking again soon. On days when you have more energy, you can stretch this routine into a longer reset, addressing the sink, taking out the trash, or loading the dish dryer. The key is to keep the window short enough that you feel a sense of completion rather than a sense of defeat for not finishing the job you started.

Consistency matters more than scope. If you miss a day, you restart the next day without guilt. A restart-friendly approach is essential for ADHD brains because it reduces the fear of starting again and helps you re-enter the rhythm quickly. To support this, you can anchor your routine to a cue you already perform. For example, stand by the sink after you brush your teeth in the evening or wash your hands after finishing a cooking task. A cue is a memory anchor; the routine is the action that follows it. When your routine becomes a consistent post-meal ritual, you'll notice the difference in your mental energy. The kitchen becomes a place of repose rather than a pressure point, and you'll find yourself choosing a small, doable action over a bigger, overwhelming goal.

The structure of a quick clean routine also benefits from a simple, predictable sequence. The order matters not because it's perfect but because it's predictable. Begin by clearing the table and collecting dishes, then wipe down the surfaces that see the most splashes, and finally put away items that are out of place. If you have a dishwasher, loading and starting it can count as part of the ritual; if not, you can rinse and place them in a designated drying rack or clean a few cups and utensils and then put them away. The sequence should feel natural, not forced, so you continue to perform it even when your energy is low. If you have kids or partners, invite them to join in a version of the routine that suits their ages and capabilities. The more the routine becomes a shared, lightweight practice, the more likely it is to persist.

Another powerful lever is the introduction of a dedicated cleaning caddy, small enough to be carried from counter to sink with ease. A caddy that contains a cloth, a bottle of mild cleaner, a sponge, and a single-purpose item such as a slim dustpan or a small brush makes the act of cleaning less intimidating. You don't have to hunt for the tools you need; they are all in one place, ready to go. The mere presence of a caddy reduces the friction to begin cleaning, and by keeping it near your primary workspace you lower the barrier to action. A routine anchored to a familiar tool is more likely to endure than a set of guidelines you memorize but never reference in the moment.

On days when energy and focus are abundant, you can expand your routine into a brief "plus" set. Wipe the sink, sweep a quick path through the floor, wipe the stove, and return everything to its place. On lean days, you'll still do the core steps: clear, wipe, tidy. The goal is to retain a core element that sticks. You don't need to do more than that to maintain a calm kitchen and a reliable rhythm. The small, repeatable routine is the secret to progress that doesn't hinge on willpower or cinematic levels of motivation. It's a quiet, trustworthy system that respects the realities of ADHD life.

In the end, quick clean routines are less about time and more about momentum. They aren't a judgment on you as a person or a measure of your worth as a homemaker. They are tools for preserving space, reducing decision fatigue, and making cleaning a non-crisis activity rather than a weekly confrontation. When you anchor your routine to clear cues, keep the actions small and repeatable, and stay flexible enough to accommodate high and low energy days, you'll find that your kitchen becomes a place you can trust again. And when the kitchen is reliable, the rest of your day follows more smoothly, with less drama and more room for the things you actually want to do.

EIGHT
PAPERWORK, MAIL, AND DIGITAL CLUTTER: A SYSTEM YOU CAN TRUST

THE MAIL TRIAGE STATION

The mail arrives and immediately begins its slow creep through the house. A flyer slips under a door, a bill lands on the counter, a catalog slides from the mailbox, and suddenly the kitchen table looks like a tiny version of a landfill. For many ADHD brains, the closest thing to a breakthrough is not the heroic sprint but the small, repeatable system that reduces the daily drama. This section gives you that system: a single, dependable mail triage station and a simple routine that keeps paper from migrating like Houdini from the hall into every room.

First, choose a spot that stays relatively quiet but is still seen every day. It should be near the point where mail enters your home, but not so isolated that it becomes out of sight and out of mind. A shallow desk tray, a small set of labeled bins, and a slim recycling container are enough to start. The surface should be easy to clear at the end of the day; you want a visible, clickable space, not a shrine to indecision. The goal is friction reduction, not a castle of folders. A compact system works better for ADHD brains because it invites you to touch the mail just once and then decide.

Set up four clear destinations within the station so you aren't forced to decide a hundred times. Incoming mail goes into the In box as a starting place. Items that require action—bills, forms to fill, notices to sign—move into an Action pile. Items you want to keep for reference, like warranties or important notices, go into an Archive or Reference tray. Anything that involves waiting on someone else—a returned form, a response from your office, a confirmation email—lands in a Waiting or Pending tray. If you need to recycle something, toss it right away, ideally without turning back to it. The label on each tray isn't a rigid law; it's a nudge to keep you moving rather than stalling in a sea of paperwork.

A key principle here is the one-touch rule. The moment you touch a piece of mail, you decide its fate. You either act on it now, set a specific plan for action and place it in Action, file it into Archive for future reference, or place a reminder in Waiting if you can't complete it yet. If something feels uncertain, you don't let it linger in a limbo state. You either assign a time-bound next step or you move it to Archive and revisit it later by a scheduled check-in. This approach reduces the cognitive drag of repeatedly re-reading the same item and the emotional energy drain of keeping everything near or around you with no clear end.

To make the station easy to live with, keep the processing time short. A 5 to 15 minute daily processing window is plenty if you've built solid habits. Use a timer not to punish yourself but to signal a brief sprint that clears the clutter, not a marathon that exhausts your patience. Begin with the most obvious items: a bill due soon, a form requiring a signature, a letter that looks like something you should keep but doesn't demand immediate action. As you practice, you'll find you naturally migrate through the space with less hesitation because the destinations are clear and the steps are small. If you miss a day, that's not a failure; it's a restart, not a rupture. The system is designed to be restarted without guilt.

The everyday life of this station is about predictability without rigidity. You don't need to decide the fate of every piece of mail in the same moment; you only need to decide which pile it belongs to and what the next step will be. Your phone or computer can become a useful ally here. A quick note to yourself about an action can be set up as a reminder in your calendar, or you can snap a photo of the item and attach a quick comment to the record in your task app. The goal is to close the gap between "I should deal with this someday" and "I've handled this today." Even when you're tired, the system should feel like a gentle funnel rather than a maze with a dozen doors you must open to move forward.

As with any ADHD-friendly system, the simplest version is often the most sustainable. Start with one tray for In, one for Action, one for Archive, and one for Waiting. If you find you've over-complicated things in your head, you can simplify by eliminating a category or merging two categories into one. The most powerful feature of the Mail Triage Station is that it creates a tiny, dependable routine that you can repeat, consistent enough to reduce anxiety even on days when motivation is low. With time, the act of handling mail becomes less daunting and more automatic, transforming the daily mail crawl into a predictable, manageable moment in your day.

SIMPLE FILING THAT DOESN'T REQUIRE PERFECTION

Filing is one of those tasks that tends to trigger perfectionism in ADHD minds. The idea of organizing every document into the perfect digital folder or color-coded cabinet can feel heroic and impossible at the same time. The truth is better than perfection here: you want fast, repeatable filing that makes sense to you and sticks. Simple filing doesn't require a grand architecture; it demands sensible, broad categories and a way to keep them accessible. When you're organizing with ADHD, the objective is to reduce the friction of looking for things later, not to build a museum of impeccably labeled bins.

Begin with a handful of broad, sturdy categories that cover most of what you'll encounter. A practical set might be Action, Reference, Archive, and Waiting. Action holds items that require you to do something, such as an insurance form, a task to complete, or a payment reminder you want to address this week. Reference is for information you might need later but don't need to act on now—warranty details, manuals, or receipts you want to keep for a time but don't want to see every day. Archive stores items you want to keep for future access or for tax and record-keeping purposes, such as tax forms, old statements, or important agreements. Waiting is where you place items that you've sent to someone else for action and are waiting for a reply.

The beauty of this approach is that it's forgiving. You don't have to decide the perfect place for every document the moment you touch it. If something feels like it doesn't fit neatly into a single category, give it a provisional home and mark a note for yourself to revisit later. You can physically label your file bins with simple words or even color-coded stickers to help you locate what you need at a glance. Keeping the process brisk is essential: one quick read, a one-line decision, and a place for the item. If you're scanning or digitizing, your scanning workflow can be integrated with your filing routine so that an image of a document lands in the right digital folder while the physical copy moves to its appropriate tray.

To make simple filing stick, pair it with a predictable time window. A short block of time, perhaps 5 to 10 minutes, once or twice a week can be enough to maintain the system. In those windows, start by gathering the day's mail and any loose papers lying around, then work through the items in order of urgency or likelihood of needing soon. As you file, avoid the trap of over-categorizing. If you're tired or distracted, you might be better off placing something in Reference and deciding later whether it belongs in Action or Waiting. The goal is to keep the system moving, not to create an obsession out of every piece of paper.

Don't be surprised if you find yourself occasionally reorganizing bins in your head. That's part of life with an ADHD brain: your habits will evolve as you learn what's actually useful. The important thing is that the core, easy-to-use framework stays intact. If you're tempted to tighten the labeling to a single word per bin, do it. If you prefer short phrases, that works too. The flexibility of this approach is its strength: it grows with you and your home, not against you. Remember that you're building a tool to reduce friction, not to trap yourself in a perfect filing system that only appears when you imagine the future you could be living.

A practical aside for home offices or shared living spaces: place your filing zone near where you sort mail, with a shallow tray or box for each category. Keep the items you touch most often within easy reach and leave less-frequent documents in a higher shelf or deeper cabinet, out of sight but accessible if needed. The moment you turn filing into a five- to ten-minute ritual that you can repeat, you'll notice a surprising drop in frantic searches, last-minute scrambles, and the guilt that often accompanies disorganization. The goal is to keep you moving, not to trap you in a never-ending minute-by-minute grading of every single document.

BILLS, DEADLINES, AND AUTOMATION

Money matters tend to command attention with unusual intensity, and for ADHD brains, the pressures of bills and deadlines can feel overwhelming even when the amounts are modest. The goal here is to tame that pressure with a system that catches due dates before they slip into the abyss, that automates routine payments where possible, and that creates dependable reminders without becoming another chore. You deserve a home where finances are clear, predictable, and not a daily source of drama. The core idea is to reduce late fees, missed availability windows, and the cognitive load of chasing deadlines by weaving automation into the fabric of your routines.

Start by collecting all the essential documents into a single, predictable flow. If you receive most bills by email, create a dedicated folder or tag in your email client and set up filters that push those messages into the folder automatically. If bills arrive by mail, keep a small pocket folder labeled with the month and place bills there as they come in. The intention is to keep every bill in sight for a finite, short period, never buried in a pile where you forget to act. From there, you can decide how to handle each item. Some bills are suitable for autopay, a tactic that eliminates the recurring decision to pay and reduces the anxiety of deadline-driven reminders. Autopay works well for utilities, subscriptions, and recurring charges you know you'll pay on time most months. If you're wary of autopay for large or variable bills, you can still automate the reminders: a calendar event with a reminder a week before the due date, another a day prior, and a final toot when it's paid. The automation itself should be simple to manage and visible enough to prevent calamity.

A practical rhythm helps: a monthly sweep to review all bills, a weekly check to confirm upcoming due dates, and a daily quick glance to catch anything that looks urgent. The weekly check becomes the moment to verify that autopays did not fail, that you have enough funds in your account, and that no receipt or invoice has slipped into the wrong folder. For many ADHD brains, automation is a form of cognitive relief—it creates a safety net that doesn't demand steady, explicit attention.

If you're managing a household with partners or roommates, consider a shared ledger or a single dashboard that the household can consult, so responsibilities are clear and not buried in individual calendars. Communicating a simple system is as important as the system itself.

When it comes to deadlines that can't be automated, such as filings or appointments, format a predictable, non-negotiable reminder cadence. A recurring event in your calendar, coupled with a short, actionable task list tied to that event, can be enough to ensure you show up on time. The idea is to reduce the sharp spikes of stress that come from last-minute scrambles. And if you forget a payment for a moment, don't punish yourself; acknowledge the oversight and use it to tune the system. Adjust the reminder cadence, change the day of the week you review, or add a second, more urgent alert. With a few small tweaks, you'll discover a rhythm that fits your energy and your schedule rather than fighting against them.

Some days you'll still forget a payment or a due date. That happens. The difference is that your system has resilience built into it. The point is not perfection but reliability. Autopay for the bills that don't require careful review, a transparent reminder system for those that do, and a routine that keeps you present with your finances without sacrificing your sense of control. In a home where ADHD is part of the equation, the right automation can become a quiet partner: it works behind the scenes, and you notice it only when it prevents a late fee or a frantic late-night search for a receipt.

If you share finances with someone else, treat financial organization as a shared project rather than a private chore. Establish a shared calendar, a shared folder for receipts and important documents, and clear boundaries about who handles what. The aim is not to police each other but to create a transparent, forgiving system that respects each person's energy and time. As you implement these steps, keep a small, flexible notebook or digital note that captures what's working and what isn't. Your system should tell you when it needs a reshaping, not demand you to start from scratch every few weeks.

DIGITAL DECLUTTER BASICS

The digital world is a different kind of clutter, but the same ADHD truths apply: it expands to fill the space you give it, grows with every new app, and vanishes if you don't give it a purpose. Digital decluttering doesn't require heroic sessions of shredding and scanning; it calls for repeatable, bite-sized steps that eventually become routine. Start with one arena at a time and finish the step you begin. The reward is not a pristine laptop but a faster, calmer workspace where you can think clearly and work with less friction.

Photos accumulate like snow in winter. They multiply with every snapshot, and many remain unseen for years. A practical approach is to move photos you truly care about into a single year-based folder and purge duplicates, near-duplicates, and blurry shots. If you're using a cloud service, use its built-in tools to identify similar images and prune them. A daily or weekly routine can be as simple as, "I'll scan my recent photos and delete the obviously unsalvageable ones, then back up the rest." The key is not to chase perfection but to reduce the overwhelm. When you finish, you should feel lighter, not more anxious about the photos you didn't touch.

Downloads are another common sinkhole. They pile up quietly because they're easy to forget and easy to ignore. A straightforward rule helps: move anything you're sure you'll need to a designated folder and delete the rest. If you're unsure, create a temporary holding folder called *To Decide* with a soft expiration date. After a short window, say seven days, you decide whether to keep or trash what's there. The trick is to keep the system portable—no heavy archiving rituals, just enough order to find the handful of necessary files when you need them.

Email often becomes the digital equivalent of a paper pile. The ADHD brain benefits from a fast, forgiving inbox policy. Try applying an 80/20 rule: 80 percent of what lands in your inbox is unremarkable and can wait, while 20 percent deserves attention today or this week. Turn off multichannel notifications to avoid constant interruptions. Set aside a specific time for email rather than checking it on every ping. Use filters to auto-sort newsletters and promotions into a separate folder, and unsubscribe from those you no longer want. A light-touch approach to email means you rarely have to face a wall of unread messages, and you can decide in a minute or two what to do with the rest.

Folder structure for digital documents can be simple and predictable. Create a top-level set of broad categories such as Personal, Finances, Work, and Receipts. Within each, use a few predictable subfolders. The goal is to have a mental map you can recall with little effort, not a sprawling taxonomy you'll never navigate. A simple approach creates an mental elbow room when deadlines loom. If you're a person who benefits from visual cues, consider color-coding folders or using icons that you connect with quickly. The moment you can locate documents in a few seconds, you've already reduced a significant chunk of mental fatigue.

Automation has a place in digital decluttering too. Use automated backups to an external drive or cloud service so you know your memories and documents aren't at risk. Filters can route newsletters out of your main inbox and into a reading folder. Auto-archive rules can move older messages into a separate history folder, where they're still accessible but not in your active field of view. The aim is to put the heavy lifting on the background where it belongs, freeing up your attention for the tasks that require your nuanced decision-making and creativity.

Finally, set a recurring, brief digital maintenance window. A 10-minute weekly ritual can keep your digital world clean without turning into an overwhelming project. In that window you can prune a small set of files, delete obvious duplicates, confirm that backups ran properly, and scan for any new items that have drifted into places they don't belong. The consistency of a tiny ritual beats the sporadic bursts of cleaning energy that are hard to sustain. You deserve a digital workspace that feels calm and efficient, not crowded and chaotic.

NINE
BEDROOMS, BATHROOMS, AND HIGH-FRICTION ZONES

BEDROOM LAUNCHPAD: START HERE

Your bedroom is more than a place to sleep. For ADHD brains, it can be the launching point for the day, or the gravity that pulls energy down every time you walk in. A space designed with momentum in mind makes it easier to do the next right thing rather than wade through a sea of decisions. Imagine a bedroom that nudges you toward the morning you want, not one that reminds you of all the tasks you didn't finish. This is the kind of space you can build with small, repeatable choices that fit your real life.

Begin with three simple zones that keep things predictable: a sleep zone around the bed, a dressing zone with a straightforward setup for clothes, and a morning-prep zone near the door for the bag, shoes, and quick essentials. The goal is to reduce friction by limiting options and arranging items so they align with how you move through your day. If you hate choosing outfits at 7 a.m., the answer isn't more outfits; it's fewer, better-chosen options that work together and stay visible.

Clothes are one of the biggest decision points in the morning. A small, consistent system can be the difference between starting the day with intention and waking up to a fog of choices. Keep a minimal wardrobe that's easy to mix and match. If your closet bursts with clothes that don't fit or haven't felt right for months, set them aside for now, and wear pieces you're confident in this week. The goal is reliability over variety: you want outfits that look decent and feel comfortable without an emotional or cognitive toll to assemble.

A hamper placed at the foot of the bed becomes an anchor for the entire clothing chain. When you discard clothes, you drop them into the hamper first, not on the chair, the floor, or the sofa. This one small placement saves you from that chaotic cascade that begins with clean clothes ending up in the wrong place. The morning flow can start the night before with a minimal ritual: lay out the outfit you've chosen for tomorrow, place the bag you'll take, set the water bottle on the dresser, and plug in any devices you need. The fewer steps you have to improvise in the morning, the more energy you save for the actual actions that matter next.

Lighting and surface organization matter just as much as the wardrobe. A calm, gentle light helps you avoid the lure of staying under the covers when you should be moving toward your day. A small tray on the dresser can hold a phone, a glass of water, and a few essentials so you're not hunting for them at dawn. The bed itself should be a sanctuary of clean lines and predictable access, not a magnet for laundry piles and clutter that shout for attention the moment you wake up. The idea is to design the bed and its surroundings so you can transition smoothly from sleep to action without an energy-draining scramble.

Consider the rhythm of your week as you plan. A quick Sunday reset doesn't have to be a long, intense process. Ten minutes to review what you'll wear, five minutes to tidy the surfaces, and a quick check of your anchor zones can set you up for a calmer week. You might create a simple habit of reviewing the next day's plan before bed and placing anything you'll need by the door. The aim is not to invent a perfect system but to create a restartable, forgiving routine that you can repeat with minimal friction.

The effect of a well-arranged bedroom extends beyond the room itself. A clean surface invites a clearer mind. A straightforward clothing system invites a calmer morning. A small, reliable landing pad invites you to do the next right thing without debate or delay. You are not seeking perfection; you are seeking a rhythm that you can sustain, season to season, year to year. In this space, you're laying the groundwork for momentum that carries you into the rest of your day with less resistance.

The moment you feel a shift—an extra minute saved here, a frustrating search avoided there—you'll notice how these small changes expand beyond the bedroom. You'll wake to a space that supports you. You'll begin to trust your capacity again because your environment is no longer actively working against you. You're building a home that responds to your brain's needs, not one that demands a battle with every morning decision.

If you're working with a partner, a roommate, or family, involve them in this design as appropriate. A shared space benefits from clear agreements about storage and routines, but the core idea remains the same: reduce friction, preserve energy, and keep the rhythm restartable. There's a quiet power in designing a bedroom that respects ADHD patterns—one that invites you to begin again with confidence rather than dread.

In practice, this means you may end up moving a few items, consolidating a dresser, or adding a simple hook near the door. It means choosing a handful of outfits and a single place for dirty clothes. It means, most of all, honoring your energy when you plan. The bedroom becomes a launchpad because it was built to propel you forward, not pull you backward. And once you feel that slow, steady pull toward action, you'll notice your mornings feel lighter, your decisions feel smaller, and your days begin with a sense of possibility rather than a sense of overwhelm.

BATHROOM RESET ROUTINES

The bathroom is a small space with outsized impact on mood and momentum. For many people with ADHD, this room becomes a choke point where small tasks balloon into a daily struggle. The goal here is not to turn hygiene into a heroic ordeal but to reframe routine as a reliable, low-friction system that works consistently, even on tough days. A calm, predictable bathroom reduces stress, supports self-care, and preserves energy for the rest of your day.

Start with a simple, two-stage approach: a daily routine that happens in the morning and another that closes the day. Each routine uses the same order of operations and a limited toolkit so you don't have to improvise or search for products when motivation is low. The core idea is to minimize decision fatigue by keeping essentials in the same place, in the same sequence, every time you use the space.

Organization begins with a clear surface policy. Clear counters invite action; clutter invites paralysis. Give every item a home, and use that home consistently. A practical rule is to keep only daily-use items on the bathroom counter and store the rest in a cabinet or bin, out of sight but easy to reach when you need it. This keeps the surface open for the tasks that matter—brushing teeth, washing face, applying moisturizer—without turning into a mini junk drawer every morning.

A simple storage strategy can be built around a few baskets or bins: one for the everyday items you reach for daily, another for backups or infrequently used products, and a third for cleaning supplies that stay in the bathroom to avoid scavenger hunts. Accessories like a small tray or lid can organize small items so they don't scatter across the counter. Labeling isn't about policing you; it's about reducing the cognitive load. A quick glance tells you exactly where something goes and where to find it next time.

The order of operations matters. Keep a consistent sequence for each morning and each evening routine. Brushing teeth, washing face, applying skincare, and rinsing with mouthwash can become an almost auto-pilot process if you don't have to decide what to do first. The same order every day lowers friction and keeps you moving forward rather than stumbling at the sink.

Two-minute rules are golden here. If you can't complete the full routine, aim to finish the most important baseline actions within two minutes: a quick brush, a rinse, a wipe-down of the sink. The point is to remove the sense of backlog. Once you've completed those steps, your brain has a tiny win and is more likely to continue the routine in the next moment rather than abandoning it altogether.

Maintaining a calm bathroom also means choosing products that minimize sensory load. Gentle scents, simple formulas, and familiar textures help reduce overwhelm. If a product's scent or packaging feels disruptive, swap it out for something that feels easier to work with. The goal is not to maximize enthusiasm but to create a space you can trust, reliably, day after day.

Finally, set a weekly micro-reset for the bathroom that doesn't require hours. A quick wipe of surfaces, a check of expiry dates, and a quick refresh of towels or rugs can be enough to preserve order without turning your bathroom into a full-blown chore. The bathroom should feel calm and usable, a place where care happens without a fight.

In this system, you're not chasing perfection; you're building a dependable routine that respects ADHD realities. You're choosing to reduce friction at the moment of use, to keep surfaces clear, to hold on to a small set of essential tools, and to finish tasks with predictable, repeatable momentum. When the bathroom becomes a reliable, easy space, you free up mental energy for more meaningful goals and easier days.

HOT SPOTS AND DROP ZONES

Halls, entryways, and shared living spaces accumulate what we call hot spots—areas where clutter seems to collect almost by gravity alone. For ADHD brains, these zones can become chronic stress points because they require repeated decisions, often in real time. The fix isn't heroic cleanup; it's creating intentional landing pads where items go, and a simple rhythm for processing them. The result is a home that feels organized without requiring heroic effort every single day.

Start by mapping the spaces you actually touch most: the front door, the coat rack, the coffee table, the sofa, the kitchen counter, and the entry to your bedroom. Look at each one and ask: where do things pile up here? Where would I benefit from a dedicated spot? The aim is to create a system that feels almost invisible because it's so consistent. A few high-visibility, low-friction zones can dramatically reduce the visible mess and the cognitive drag that comes with it.

A single landing pad near the door for keys, wallet, and phone can transform your ability to depart on time. A second pad near the living room can hold mail, receipts, and current paperwork or shopping lists. In the kitchen, a compact tray or basket becomes the drop zone for grocery lists, mail, and small purchases that otherwise drift around the space. A third pad near your bedroom can catch items that need action before bed—glasses, a charging cable, a book you intend to finish or return to a shelf later.

The design principle here is clear: every landing pad should be small, contained, and easy to reach. The height and location must align with how you move through the space; nothing should require a detour, a climb, or a special trip. Size matters—too large a tray invites clutter; too small a tray becomes useless. A simple rule: if you can't drop something on it in a single step, it's not a good fit for that zone. There should be a natural flow from drop to processing to put away.

Anchoring these zones with a minimal set of tools makes them even more reliable. A slim basket for mail, a hook for keys, a shallow tray for loose change or receipts—these are small items with outsized impact. The goal is to reduce the number of times you have to decide where to put something. Fewer decisions equal less fatigue, and less fatigue means you're more likely to follow through.

If you share space with others, set boundaries in a practical, non-punitive way. Agree on which items belong on each pad and how often they should be emptied or reviewed. The right boundaries don't punish; they simplify. A well-designed landing pad system also supports you when your energy is low. It's a simple, visible reminder that helps you stay on track rather than drift into a pile of things that don't belong anywhere.

The payoff is obvious in the long run: the entryway feels calmer, navigation around the home becomes clearer, and the last-minute scramble before leaving the house fades away. You'll spend less time redirecting items that drift and more time actually moving through your day with intention. The hot spots lose their gravity, and the space begins to feel like a habitat that works with you rather than against you.

TOOLS WHERE YOU USE THEM

One of the most powerful adjustments for ADHD organizing is the strategic placement of cleaning tools. The goal is to erase the scavenger-hunt ritual that often gnaws at energy and chop away at the momentum you've built. When tools are already where you need them, cleaning becomes a quick, almost automatic action rather than a drama of gathering supplies from multiple rooms.

Think of your home as a series of micro-work zones, each with a compact kit tailored to the tasks most likely there. In the kitchen, keep a small cleaning caddy under the sink or on a shelf—one spray, one sponge, one microfiber cloth, a roll of paper towels, and a trash bag tucked in the side. In the bathroom, have a separate kit with a spray bottle, a microfiber cloth, a scrub pad, and a spare roll of restroom tissue. In the bedroom or living spaces, a slim kit can contain a small duster or wipes for quick surfaces and a lint roller for fabrics, plus a trash bag or a small bin liner to tackle quick disposals.

A key principle is multi-use and lightweight design. Choose cleaning products that can handle several surfaces without changing tools. Multipurpose sprays, a single microfiber cloth that stays damp enough for a wipe but not so wet it streaks, and a compact squeegee for glass and mirrors can cover a broad range of tasks with less cognitive overhead. The fewer tools you need to manage, the less mental energy you spend deciding what to use when a space feels messy.

Placement matters as much as the tools themselves. Store the kitchen kit under the sink or in a high-traffic cabinet where you won't forget it. In the bathroom, keep your kit behind the cabinet door or on a bathroom shelf that's easy to reach before you start cleaning. The goal is to make grabbing the kit the simplest possible action, so you're more likely to do the job before your energy dips or your attention wanders.

The rhythm you create around cleaning tools should support restartability. It's okay if you forget a kit occasionally; that's not a failure, it's feedback. When you notice you've started scavenging, pause, and recall the habit you're building: a predictable place for supplies, a predictable routine for cleaning. Refill reminders can be gentle prompts, such as leaving a note on the bathroom mirror or setting a calendar reminder that aligns with your weekly reset. The point is to build a system that can restart quickly after a lapse.

The real payoff is consistency without punishment. When your tools live in their intended places and you're relying on a minimal, reliable set, cleaning stops being a crisis response and becomes a regular, manageable activity. You'll notice yourself starting sooner, stopping sooner, and moving more smoothly between tasks. And when your home supports that pattern, it becomes easier to maintain across seasons, job changes, or shifts in energy. The environment, in short, becomes your ally rather than your adversary, and that shift changes the conversation you have with your own capacity.

TEN
LIVING WITH OTHERS: SHARED SPACES, BOUNDARIES, AND AGREEMENTS

NAMING THE PROBLEM WITHOUT BLAME

When two or more people share a space the room for friction expands. For many adults with ADHD the strain does not begin with laziness or a lack of care. It starts with the way motivation shifts, the way attention can skitter away, and the way time feels elastic or sudden. In these moments a single dish pile can feel like a verdict rather than a signal. The first move is to separate the person from the mess. It is a simple shift, but it changes who gets to contribute and how they will feel while contributing. Instead of labeling the situation as a personal flaw, we frame it as a recurring pattern that involves choices, spaces, and rhythms. This is about the environment and the moment; not about a person being good or bad.

We talk in terms of patterns and needs. The pattern is that after meals, dishes accumulate and the sink fills; the counter can become a landing pad for papers or laundry; surfaces invite dust when attention is waning. The need is for a space that feels controllable again, with time cues that fit how the ADHD brain works. Language matters here. we choose words that reflect what is happening rather than who is at fault. This means swapping blame for clarity, swapping shame for strategy, and swapping excuses for a plan that works in real life. The goal is not perfection but reliability and relief. When a space feels overwhelming, people shut down; when a space feels navigable, people begin again.

A practical way to start is to observe together without judgment. Spend a few moments noting specific, observable patterns rather than judgments about character. For example, rather than saying the sink is a disaster, you can describe what you notice in neutral terms: the sink fills after meals, the dish rack is full, the drying towels are damp and scattered. Then translate those observations into shared intentions. Instead of a list of who should do what, frame the goal as a joint project with a clear next step for both people. The power of this approach lies in turning blame into information, and information into choice. ADHD minds move quickly when they feel they can control the next action, and they move more sluggishly when the action feels too big or too vague.

To turn naming into action, try a simple exercise that you can repeat as needed. Pick three recurring moments in your shared space where friction appears. Describe each with neutral language that names the pattern rather than indexing a person. Then identify a next right action that takes less than five minutes to begin and that could meaningfully reduce the friction. The next right step should be concrete, specific, and doable in a moment of high or low energy. For example, the next right step after noticing that the sink fills after meals could be a five minute rinse and place into a dish rack, followed by a plan to finish loading the dishwasher later if possible. This approach keeps momentum real while honoring the variability of ADHD energy and attention.

This work reduces shame and increases agency. When both people feel seen, they become more willing to share their own needs and limits. It is amazing how much collaboration grows when the first conversation is about patterns and not about personalities. You are not asking for perfection; you are asking for a practical process you can restart tomorrow if needed. And restart you will, because ADHD itself is a cycle of starts, resets, and new starts. Naming the problem without blame creates a neutral playing field where both people can show up as teammates rather than as critics or judges.

CLEAN ENOUGH, NOT PERFECT: SHARED STANDARDS YOU CAN LIVE WITH

Shared spaces demand shared standards, but the key is to keep those standards achievable and flexible. The goal is clean enough, not pristine, because ADHD minds rarely perform best under the pressure of a perfect standard that changes with the weather and the mood. A clean enough contract is a living document that acknowledges energy fluctuations, time pressures, and the fact that people forget things. It protects both individuals and the space by setting a realistic baseline and a plan for when the baseline feels out of reach.

The place to start is in one or two common spaces. Pick a kitchen and a living area, since these are the spaces that often set the tone for the rest of the home. In each space, agree on what clean enough looks like. For the kitchen, clean enough might mean that counters are clear enough to prepare a meal, the sink is not overflowing, and dishes are placed in the dish rack or dishwasher so the surface is available for cooking. It does not imply a sanitizer sprint, a spotless backsplash, or a completely empty sink. For the living room, clean enough could mean that cushions are arranged, clutter is contained to a single basket or shelf, and surfaces are free of obvious waste or paper piles. The aim is to reduce friction, not to trap anyone in a never ending cycle of micromanagement.

Once you have a sense of what clean enough means, write a short contract that captures this. A living contract feels different from a chore chart because it is a mutual agreement rather than a set of duties assigned to one person. The contract should name the spaces, state the standard in practical terms, and specify who does what in a way that honors both energy and preference. For ADHD friendly homes, it helps to frame the contract with a time context. You can state that the standard should be met by the end of the day for quick-turn spaces, or by a specific block of time that suits your rhythms if evenings are chaotic. The contract should also include how you handle days when energy or time is terribly short. A simple clause can say that if a day slips away, you revisit the standard the next day rather than letting it become a rule that nobody can meet.

To keep the contract usable, place it where both can easily access it and review it together once a week or when mood or schedule changes. A short one to two sentence revision after each review keeps it flexible and non punitive. You may find that you need to lower the standard for a period or reframe what counts as clear space. That is not failure; it is responsiveness. The power of clean enough lies in its simplicity and its repeatability. If both partners can say yes to the spirit of the contract, the day to day friction reduces and the space begins to breathe again. In ADHD life, agreements that feel fair and straightforward are the agreements that survive the twists of energy, time, and attention.

As you move from naming to agreement, remember the core principles. Clarity beats ambiguity, and practicality beats ambition. The contract should reflect practical routines you can perform, not heroic efforts you hope to sustain. Keep it short, keep it concrete, and keep it revisitable. The moment you feel resentful is the moment to pause and renegotiate. The goal is not to police each other but to maintain a shared environment that supports both people and the ADHD brain that lives there. A well crafted contract creates a safety net that catches missed days and invites a quick return to the steady rhythm you both want. That steadiness is what reduces the cycle of shame and burnout and makes everyday living with another person feel possible again.

PLAY TO STRENGTHS: TASK DIVISION THAT FITS YOU

In a shared home the instinct to divide chores the same way we might have learned in school can feel familiar, even comforting. But those traditional divisions often ignore how ADHD changes energy, focus, and time perception. A strengths based approach to task division begins with a simple inventory: what tasks feel easier or more natural at this moment, and who tends to perform best when energy is high versus when it is dipping. The aim is not fairness in a rigid sense but fairness in a sustainable, humane sense. Fairness becomes not a tally of minutes but a balance of energy, autonomy, and relief from repetitive stress. When tasks are matched to what people actually enjoy or can tolerate, compliance improves and resentment drops.

Start by listing the tasks that keep the shared spaces functional. You do not need to perform a scholarly analysis here; a practical, honest snapshot will do. Then rate each task by two dimensions: energy cost and cognitive load. Energy cost captures how physically and mentally demanding the task is in a given moment. Cognitive load reflects how many steps or decisions are required. With ADHD, some tasks that seem simple on the surface become draining in real life and vice versa. After you have your quick map, pair or group tasks with people who bring certain strengths to each category. A person who enjoys order and rhythm may naturally take on counter organization and routine tidy ups, while another who dislikes repetition might prefer planning and setting up a simple rotation that keeps the routine from becoming a bore.

This is not a call to create a perfect plan that never changes. It is an invitation to design a system that adapts. A key concept is a task bank, a reservoir of small, discrete actions that can be drawn from as energy permits. Each person can pick a task from the bank that they feel competent to handle at that moment. For ADHD brains, a five minute task is better than a drag of a bigger one. If you can start a five minute task and carry momentum to a longer chunk, you have succeeded more than if you forced a longer sprint that ends in shutdown. Short, repeatable tasks are easier to maintain and easier to restart when life throws a curveball.

Rotations can preserve fairness while acknowledging that capacity shifts over days and weeks. Set a gentle cadence that feels doable. A weekly rotation is often sufficient; you can also implement a two to three week cycle for more complex routines. The important thing is to keep the system visible and simple. A shared calendar or a small whiteboard in a common area can remind everyone who is responsible for what in the upcoming period, but the key is to keep the record small and legible. If someone misses a rotation or a task, the immediate response is not blame but a quick reallocation that respects current energy levels and commitments. It is crucial to preserve agency. Everyone should feel they have a voice in deciding where they contribute and how they grow.

Some practical guidelines help this approach work in the long run. Start with a small set of tasks that are clearly defined and quick to complete. Use a next right step framework to reduce overwhelm. The next right step is the smallest action that can reasonably be taken to advance the larger goal. For example, a kitchen task bank might include a one minute wipe of the counter to clear space for cooking, followed by a five minute loading of the dishwasher, followed by a plan to run the dishwasher at a specific time. If a person notices that a task is not feasible at the moment, they can choose a different task from the bank that better matches their energy level. A simple rotation schedule helps people stay aligned without lingering resentment, because each person knows what to expect and has input into the order of tasks.

The practical reward of this approach is visible. Chores stop feeling like punitive reminders of failure and start feeling like options that fit a live, evolving routine. When you step into a task that matches your energy and your capacity for decision, you are more likely to begin and to continue. You do not need to wait for a perfect day to make progress. You only need to take the next right step and let the system absorb the variability that ADHD brings. Over time, this shifts the dynamic from a tug of war to a collaboration where both people feel seen, respected, and able to contribute in ways that honor their unique brains.

THE SUPPORT TOOLKIT: BODY DOUBLING, CHECK-INS, AND REMINDERS

A shared home can feel calmer when you borrow a few adaptable supports from ADHD friendly communities. The first is body doubling. The presence of another person while you start a task can drastically reduce the inertia that often follows a long planning phase or a blocked start. Body doubling does not require long sessions or constant attention. It is about proximity and timing. In a living situation, you can schedule a short window where a partner sits in the kitchen while you put away groceries, or you join a friend via video chat while you clear a cluttered shelf. The goal is to share the experience of starting, not to monitor every move. When energy is limited or attention is scattered, that silent companionship can be a powerful nudge to begin and to sustain momentum. For some people, the physical presence is empowering; for others, a light, asynchronous presence works better. The key is to tailor the arrangement to what feels supportive rather than coercive.

Check-ins are a second pillar of support. They should be brief, structured, and optional. A check-in can occur at a set time each day or week, and it should aim to surface two things: what you started and what you need to keep going. The questions should be concrete and action oriented rather than interpretive. How is the space today for you? What would help you in the next 24 hours to move one useful thing forward? Is there a small task you want to claim or pass to someone else? Keep the format predictable, and keep it kind. Check-ins are experiences of mutual care, not audits. If a check-in becomes a source of pressure, it is time to pause and adjust the cadence or format so that the practice remains helpful rather than controlling.

Reminders address a common ADHD challenge: memory. Visual cues, timers, and simple prompts can turn intention into action. Place reminders in highly visible locations and align them with natural routines. A sticky note on the fridge that marks the end of the day tasks, a timer set to the moment you plan to begin, or a calendar alert that pings at the same time each morning can all serve as gentle prompts rather than nagging. The simplest reminders are the ones you trust to prompt you at the right moment rather than the ones you resent seeing every day. Build a reminder system that respects both energy and autonomy. If you forget, you do not fail; you simply restart with a new cue or a new arrangement.

All three strategies work best when they are consensual and flexible. No one should feel that they are being watched or controlled. Instead, the goal is to cultivate a sense of collaboration and shared momentum. With body doubling you create space to begin; with check-ins you sustain accountability in a warm and practical way; with reminders you reduce friction in memory. The result is a living support system that travels with the rhythms of life in a home, not a rigid set of rules that feel punitive on a bad day. This approach acknowledges how ADHD shows up for each person and honors the fact that supportive structures must be resets, renewals, and reimaginings as seasons change. And when a system needs tweaking, you talk about it openly, you adjust the expectations, and you continue forward with care.

A RESTARTABLE HOME AND A KINDER RELATIONSHIP WITH CLEANING

YOUR PERSONALIZED TOOLKIT

This is where the work from the last pages becomes a living thing you can pick up tomorrow morning, afternoon, or whenever life suddenly tilts. A toolkit is not a shiny checklist you never touch. It's a small, reliable collection of strategies that fits your energy, your schedule, and your pace. It lives inside your home and inside your head, ready to be used when you need it most. The goal isn't to build a perfect system but to build a flexible one that reduces friction, invites you to start, and stays usable when motivation wanes. When you picture your toolkit, imagine a drawer that actually opens without a fight, a routine that feels like a helpful nudge rather than a steel rod pressing down on you. Your toolkit should feel liberating, not punitive.

First, focus on the routines that fit your energy after a long day or after a rough morning. A toolkit that assumes you have a full tank every day will fail you. Instead, design with energy limits in mind. If mornings are crowded with competing needs, you might anchor with a tiny 5-minute kitchen reset or a 10-minute clothes pick-up. If afternoons are your most wired time, you could schedule a 15-minute declutter sprint or a quick paper catch-up. The point is to choose routine blocks that are short enough to begin without stalling out your entire day, yet concrete enough to finish with something visible and real.

Second, build your task-chunking language. A task should always have a single, Next Right Step. That means you move from vague chores like "tidy up" to something you can start in a moment: open the laundry basket by the bed and pull out a single load, or stand in the kitchen and rinse the sink. The power of one small action is that it creates momentum, not guilt. When you pair that first action with a tiny reward or a reassuring reminder—something as simple as a breath or a sip of water—you've turned a potentially overwhelming moment into a discreet victory. This is how you fight decision fatigue: you reduce choices to one obvious next move and let that move lead you forward.

Third, shape your environment to remove friction. Clutter often wins when it forces you to hunt for a place, a tool, or a surface. Your toolkit includes tiny environmental tweaks, like placing a dedicated laundry basket in a convenient corner, labeling a "go-to" bin for paperwork that actually makes sense, or setting a routine cue that travels with you from room to room. You're not chasing perfection; you're creating spaces that invite you to act instead of freeze. Think about the places you stall—kitchen counters, the space by the front door, the desk—and ask what one small change would make it easier to do the next thing.

Fourth, embed recognition and repair into your toolkit. You'll have days when nothing goes as planned, and that's not a moral failing. It's a data point. Your toolkit should include a gentle repair plan: a ten-minute reset, a buddy check-in, a note to yourself that says, "Today is a reset, not a failure." The ability to restart without shame is the core of a healthy relationship with cleaning. When you anticipate setbacks and prepare a kinder reply to them, you remove the dread that sabotages your best intentions.

Finally, keep your toolkit kid-and-roommate friendly. If you share spaces with others, you'll want your strategy to be understandable and doable for everyone involved. You might adapt routines into shared rituals that respect different rhythms and capacities. A toolkit that only works when one person is perfectly aligned is not a toolkit for real homes. The happiest, most sustainable setups are those that invite cooperation without turning into a parent-child dynamic. You deserve a home that feels cooperative, not punitive.

To begin shaping your personalized toolkit today, imagine your next clean, calm moment in a space you care about. What small action would make that moment possible? What one habit, repeated for a week, would reduce the most friction? Write down one next right step you're willing to try tomorrow, and another for the day after if you feel up to it. Your toolkit is a compass, not a map to a perfect destination. It will grow as life changes, seasons shift, and energy waxes or wanes. It is yours to adjust, to reframe, and to rely on when you feel overwhelmed. And because it is built around your real patterns, it is far more likely to last than a grand, one-size-fits-all plan. Style it to your life, and give it room to breathe.

THE RESTART PLAN FOR MESSY WEEKS

Setbacks are not the opposite of progress; they are a part of it. The Restart Plan is your gentle protocol for reclaiming ground after chaos, burnout, or a too-long stretch of "not today." It's a simple, repeatable sequence you can rely on when you wake up to a counter full of chores you can't face. The essence of the plan is to reduce the distance between "I can start now" and "I did something that matters." The steps below read like a story you tell yourself in moments of hesitation, a narrative voice that invites you to try again rather than berate yourself.

Begin with acknowledgment. When you notice you've slipped, name the moment without judgment. Say to yourself something like, "That happened. Tonight I'll reset. I'm choosing a small start." Acknowledgment is not permission to wallow; it's a brief, honest check-in that frees you from carrying guilt as you move forward. Then pick a single, measurable start point. It should be tiny but concrete—like "start the dishwasher and wipe the sink for five minutes" or "put away two cups in the drying rack and straighten the counter." The aim is to begin with a task that requires less than ten minutes of focus but yields a verifiable win.

Next, set a time anchor. Choose a window—ten minutes, fifteen, or a fixed period tied to a current energy level. The timer is not a punishment; it's a boundary that helps your brain commit to a finite effort and know when it's time to pause or stop. As you begin, notice the friction you encounter and name it. Is it decision fatigue about which item goes where, a mental block about where to start, or a distraction that keeps pulling you away? Identifying the friction helps you craft a more precise restart next week. If the friction is too big to overcome in the allotted time, you adjust the scope: you reduce to five minutes or switch to a different area with a clearer starting point.

The restart plan also requires a tiny ritual to signal the reset moment. It could be turning on a lamp, putting on a favorite song for a short burst of work, or a simple breath cue that tells your brain, "We are starting now." Rituals are powerful because they turn a cognitive nudge into a physical cue. They reduce the mental energy required to begin and help your attention settle on the task at hand. After you complete the chosen task, pause to observe what happened. You might note in a small journal or a quick note on your phone what you accomplished and how you felt. The act of recording a win, no matter how small, reinforces the idea that starting is possible, even when life feels busy or unpredictable.

Finally, close the loop with a quick assessment and a revised plan. Ask: Did I complete the next right step? If yes, great. If not, what's the smallest next move I can take in the next session? This is not perfectionism in disguise; it is a process of continuous adjustment that acknowledges that some days you'll need to scale back and others you'll surprise yourself with momentum. The Restart Plan is a living blueprint that respects your rhythm. It is meant to be revisited, adjusted, and possibly simplified as life changes—from a busy work season to a quieter home stretch, from a new baby to a move or a new roommate. You carry it with you because it has proven helpful in a thousand tiny moments, and those moments add up to a home that actually feels manageable over time.

In practice, the plan becomes a short series of resets you can perform on autopilot. You don't need a perfect storm of good conditions to start; you need a single, doable action that signals you're in the game again. That action could be as simple as placing one bin by the door for incoming mail, turning on the light in the hallway, or pulling a single garment from a chair and folding it on a nearby surface. Each restart builds trust with yourself. It's not about a flawless record; it's about a growing ability to recover swiftly and without condemnation.

The Restart Plan is not a punishment for having a messy week. It is a compassionate invitation to re-engage with your space, your energy, and your own capacity to create order you can maintain. If you have a partner, a friend, or a coach who checks in with you, this plan gives them a simple language for support, not judgment. The plan respects your pace, honors your limits, and reminds you that every renewed effort is a win worth noting. The more you use it, the louder the message becomes: you are capable of starting again, and you deserve a home that supports that start, not one that shames you for needing it.

To make it your own, rehearse the Restart Plan when you're doing well as well as when you're not. The more you practice returning to a small, reachable beginning, the more your brain learns to respond with curiosity instead of resistance. You'll start to notice a quiet but steady shift: a sense that you can sustain small, meaningful changes even during busy or stressful periods. The Restart Plan is your invitation to rebuild momentum, not to chase impossible perfection, and that distinction changes the entire experience of keeping a home with ADHD.

Measuring success with this plan is not about counting spotless counters; it's about recognizing that the ability to begin again is, in itself, a valuable skill. A restart is a reset that protects your energy for the bigger tasks you do want to tackle. In time, the plan becomes second nature: a familiar routine that reduces the cognitive load that so often holds you back. You'll find a renewed sense of control, and with it, a calmer sense of possibility that you can carry into every week, every month, and every new season of life.

MEASURING SUCCESS DIFFERENTLY

If you've spent years chasing the dream of a perfectly clean home, you're not alone. The real magic of this chapter is learning to measure progress in a language that matches your brain and your life. It isn't about spotless counters or a flawless routine; it's about stress reduction, recovery, and the quiet, practical wins that stack up over days, weeks, and months. When you measure success differently, you invite a kinder, more honest relationship with cleaning—one that credits effort, not perfection, and that recognizes how much energy you have on a given day.

Start with a simple question: how stressed were you by the end of today's chores? Imagine a scale from 0 to 10, where 0 means the day felt calm and 10 means you felt overwhelmed. This is not a punishment scale; it's a tool to understand your own cycles. If you notice your stress tends to spike during a certain time of day or with certain tasks, you can plan around that pattern. You'll learn to reserve your strongest energy for the tasks that matter most and choose lighter, maintenance-oriented tasks when your energy dips. Over time, you'll see a trend: fewer 9s and 10s, more mid-range days where you can complete a small, meaningful chunk and call it a win.

Another useful measure is recoverability. How quickly can you bounce back after a setback? Do you find you can drop the weight of a missed day and come back with a tiny reset, or do you spiral into guilt and delay? The more quickly you recover, the more you're building resilience into your life. Track recovery time in your journal or a note on your phone—how long after a disruption does it take you to re-engage with a task and finish something you care about? The goal isn't to erase the disruptions but to shorten the downtime between them and the next action that matters.

Consider the clarity of your environment as a metric. Clarity is not about perfection; it's about how easy it is to start tomorrow. Do you arrive in the morning and immediately know where the next right step lives? Is there a surface that stays clear enough to prepare a simple breakfast? Do you have a reliable place for mail, papers, and digital tasks that prevents piles from taking over? As you tune your space to minimize friction, you'll notice how much easier it is to act. This is not about seeing every item in perfect order; it's about recognizing how quickly you can move from intent to action.

Measure time gained and lost in a way that fits your life. If you're constantly chasing time you don't have, you'll miss the real value of progress. Instead, track small boundaries you create and respect: the 10-minute timer that helps you finish a task, the 5-minute morning reset that makes breakfast feasible, the 15-minute evening tidy that helps you sleep with a calmer mind. When you review these moments, you'll notice a pattern: progress doesn't require long, heroic sessions. It requires consistent, bite-sized action that you can sustain and repeat.

Then consider the emotional weight you carry into the next day. Do you wake up with a lighter sense of obligation, or is the day already crowded with reminders of unfinished tasks? If your mood lightens after you complete a small routine, that is a meaningful success. The goal is to feel more capable, not to check every item off a list. You're building a life that can absorb irregular days without breaking your overall trajectory. Your success, finally, is the reduction of hesitation, the increase in confidence that you can begin again, and the consistent ability to recover when life doesn't go as planned.

A practical way to implement this is to keep a simple, reflective record. Note the one metric you care about most—stress, recoverability, clarity, or time gained—and track it for a few weeks. You'll likely notice a pattern: when you attend to your energy and reduce friction, your chosen metric improves. It's a feedback loop that teaches you what truly matters in your home and your life. The most powerful measure is not how clean the space is, but how you feel in your space. When your home supports your best days rather than amplifying your worst, you've achieved a form of success that lasts far longer than any one cleaning spree.

Finally, celebrate the small moments with curiosity rather than judgment. If you finished a small task and felt a sigh of relief flood your body, that's a win worth recording. If you reset a space and found yourself surprised by how much easier the next task became, that's evidence of momentum. The aim is to cultivate a way of living where progress is visible, repeatable, and forgiving. You'll make fewer promises you can't keep and keep more promises you can, to yourself and to the people you share your home with. Measuring success this way turns cleaning from a performance into a practice, one that respects your needs and celebrates your consistent, imperfect, human rhythm.

KEEPING THE MOMENTUM WITH SUPPORT

Momentum grows when you invite others to walk with you rather than criticise you from the sidelines. In a home that works for ADHD, support isn't about policing behavior; it's about shared clarity, mutual respect, and practical collaboration. Keeping the momentum means building a network that sustains your progress through the ordinary chaos of life: the unpredictable work shifts, the sudden guests, the flu that knocks everyone off schedule, and the ordinary days that make you wonder if you'll ever catch up. Your support system can be a mix of accountability partners, trusted friends, family members, a coach or therapist, and perhaps a community group that shares your goals. The key is to make support specific, reliable, and kind.

Begin with clear boundaries and agreements that honor everyone's capacity. If you live with a partner or roommates, a shared space benefits from explicit understandings about expectancies and responsibilities. The aim is not to split chores according to a parent-child dynamic but to distribute tasks in a way that respects each person's rhythm and skill. You might agree on a simple cadence for shared spaces: a quick daily check-in, a weekly reset, and a flexible approach to larger projects that accommodates days when someone is too tired or overwhelmed. The agreements should be revisited with curiosity, not with shame or blame, and they should be written in language that both of you can understand and remember.

Professional help has a crucial role too. An ADHD coach or therapist can offer strategies tailored to your brain's patterns and help you translate the book's concepts into your daily life. A coach can keep you accountable in practical ways—setting expectations, reviewing progress, and reframing setbacks as data rather than judgments. Support groups and communities provide a sense of belonging and practical ideas you can borrow, adapt, and improve. They remind you you're not alone and that many people are learning the same lessons, sometimes at different speeds.

Support also means protecting your space from your own worst impulses. You deserve a home that meets you where you are, not a space that leaves you feeling judged or exhausted. This might mean arranging for a friend to drop by for a ten-minute help session, setting up a shared digital board where chores are visible and updates are easy, or scheduling regular, predictable times for routine maintenance that don't overwhelm your calendar. When support is anchored in respect, you gradually see a shift in how you feel about cleaning. It becomes something you do with others, not something you do to yourself.

To sustain momentum, cultivate small, regular rituals that involve the people around you. A weekly 20-minute family reset, a calendar reminder for a 5-minute check-in after dinner, or a standing plan to prep a few meals together can transform a once-stressful routine into something you anticipate. The idea is to create a rhythm you can count on, a rhythm that protects your energy and makes your home feel predictable in a good way. You'll still have off days. You'll still forget a load of laundry or misplace a bill. But with support, you'll experience the same moments as everyone else: the chance to start again, the relief that comes with a shared plan, and the confidence that you're building something sustainable rather than chasing a fantasy of perfect order.

Your home will never be perfectly finished, and that is not the goal. The goal is continuation: a steady, reachable path that respects your ADHD rather than fighting it. Support helps you stay on that path without burning out. It offers you a safety net that is sturdy enough to catch you but flexible enough to let you move. When you know you have someone to confide in, a routine that makes sense for all of you, and access to professionals who can help tailor the approach, your momentum becomes less fragile. It becomes a shared, ongoing practice rather than a solitary struggle.

As you picture the future of your home, see it as restartable and resilient. The chapters you just finished are not the end; they are the foundation for your ongoing life with ADHD. You can return to your toolkit, revisit your restart plan, and tweak your measurements as life changes. You can adjust your support networks, negotiate new boundaries, and still keep the core idea intact: you deserve a home that supports you, a relationship with cleaning that is kinder, and a daily life that doesn't rely on perfection but on sustainable, compassionate momentum. The chapter you've reached is a doorway, not a wall. Step through with curiosity, and you'll discover that sustainable progress isn't a destination. It's a practice you can repeat, adapt, and renew again and again.

www.ingramcontent.com/pod-product-compliance
Lightning Source LLC
Chambersburg PA
CBHW071346080526
44587CB00017B/2981